DEDICATION: To my daughters: Brandi, April and Angie. Of all the blessings in my life, I thank our Lord the most for you.

AUTHOR
Alicia Larson

EDITOR: Sheri Wright

PHOTOGRAPHER: David Schultz

CRYSTAL IMAGES
(719)-661-0167
FAX (719)-481-8930

TABLE OF CONTENTS

INTRODUCTION

This book has been many years in the writing; I started writing it fifteen years ago, when I was taking glass lessons myself. I was so frustrated with my teacher, the glass, the cuts, and my own lack of natural talent, that I wanted to quit many times. It was this frustration that first prompted me to write a book that could simplify the art and techniques of Stained Glass...and spare others the frustration that I had to overcome. The good news is that you don't need "natural talent". You can be very good at stained glass with the lessons in this book, lots of practice and good old fashioned tenacity. This book is for all those who want to learn, and especially those that have tried and tried...and are ready to succeed!

HOW TO USE THIS MANUAL

IF YOU ARE NOT IN A CLASS

This is a manual in the truest sense. Think of it as a teacher on paper. It is important that you decide NOW to make it through to the end of the book. Keep in mind that if it were easy, it wouldn't be worth learning. Remember the first time you drove a car with a clutch? Looking back on it, most of us felt like quitting and punching the person trying to teach us. You might as well know that you will probably get mad at the glass too, and that in a few weeks most of the techniques will come naturally. Important, also, is that you do EVERY part of each lesson. Repeat the lessons if necessary, until you understand the procedures without having to refer to the book. This does not mean that you have to be an expert before moving on, just that you feel comfortable practicing that particular step.

PRACTICE!!! Your life is already full, and you must declare a time for nothing but glass. A half hour a day is not much to ask for this incredible skill. I guarantee that you will succeed with practice, and I know you won't without it!

IF YOU ARE IN A CLASS

Or, if you are already skilled in Stained Glass, I suggest that you read through each lesson, and try anything that sounds new to you. Many of the techniques in this book have never been published before, and you will find them useful as a supplement to your instructors lessons. REMEMBER: There are many methods and techniques in Stained Glass, and no manual contains them all. Your instructors methods will be their own; take advantage of their knowledge and use this book for coaching.

IF YOU GET STUCK

Use the Trouble Shooting Guide and Glossary at the back of the book. If that doesn't help, take a break and start fresh later; it really does help!

LESSON ONE:
LEARNING TO CUT

G o shopping! This does not have to be very expensive, and I wouldn't ask you to do such a strenuous thing if it weren't necessary. You may already have some of these materials, so gather those up and buy the rest. I have listed the supplies according to the lesson they are first used in, so you have the option of buying over time. The list is followed by a description of each item. Most of these tools are available at stained glass stores. Look in the phone book under "Glass, Stained and Leaded" It's usually right after "Glass, Auto". Here's your list:

SUPPLIES:

STAINED GLASS SUPPLIER

Glass cutter
Cutting oil
Grozing and/or "Perfect Bite" pliers
Safety glasses
X-acto type knife, #1
#11 X-acto blades
Stained Glass for each pattern
Lead came 3/16 H
Lead Vice
Copper Foil 7/32 and 1/4 in.
Zinc Came 1/4 in U
Lead Cutters
Glass Grinder**
A grid for cutting (Morton)*
Soldering Iron
Flux, liquid and paste
Soldering Stand
Fid*
Foiling Shears
Wire brush*
60/40 Solder
Grey DAP 33 putty
Patina

White craft paper
Black fine felt tip
Sharpie med. point (black)
Small jar
Masking tape 1 in.
Spray adhesive
Wire cutters
Plywood, 2 ft X 2 ft.
Wood strips
Nails
Horse shoe nails
Galvanized Steel or Copper Wire
Claw Hammer
L-Square
Metal Ruler
Rubber gloves
Plaster of Paris 1/2 lb
Natural bristle scrub brush
Paper towels
Solder Syringe or Wick*
Nail brush
Pencil
Cellulose Sponges

Light Box*
Flux Brush
Flux Remover

Window glass scraps
<u>Stained Glass *Design* Secrets</u>

These are the bare essentials for working in stained glass. Other tools may be mentioned in the text, which you may want to acquire as you increase your involvement in stained glass .

*These items may be purchased as you need them. You will benefit from having each tool listed.

**A grinder is a very important tool, though the most expensive one listed. Local stained glass suppliers may rent you time on their grinders until you can purchase your own. A sickle stone is an inexpensive tool that can be used for minor edge grinding.

DESCRIPTION OF SUPPLIES

LESSONS 1 - 4

A GLASS CUTTER: Please get a simple cutter...nothing fancy, with or without a ball tip for your first practice lessons. (If all you have is an old one in the bottom of a drawer somewhere, buy a new one). This cutter will probably be ruined by the time you finish lesson four (beginners are hard on cutters!) When you start your first project, **get a good quality, self oiling cutter.** The better quality cutters can save you a lot of broken glass from bad cuts!

WHITE PAPER: 12 to 24 inches is a good width, and you will use up to 24 ft. Art stores sell inexpensive white (craft) paper by the roll. Some grocery stores will sell you white butcher paper for a minimal amount. When you get very productive with your new art form, you can buy large rolls of unwaxed white paper from paper and box suppliers.

CUTTING OIL: You can substitute turpentine instead, but it's not water soluble and leaves more residue on the glass.

GROZING PLIERS: This is one item that you should splurge on. It really helps to have two *quality* pairs. I like the new "Perfect Bite" Plier for it's versitility, but I also use grozers.

BLACK FELT TIP PEN (FINE POINT): Yes, it must be black and it must be felt tip (not roller tip).

A "SHARPIE": Medium point permanent marker.

SMALL JAR WITH LID: If you know any babies...

MASKING TAPE: 1" wide.

SPRAY ADHESIVE: Any photo-mount type spray.

A PIECE OF PLYWOOD AND/OR WORKTABLE: Plywood scraps (not particle board, it's too dense and heavy) from construction sites are great. They must be large enough to use as a cutting surface (2 ft. x 2 ft. is a nice size). If you have a worktable, be aware that the surface will get scratched if you don't put a piece of plywood on top of it.

ANOTHER PIECE OF PLYWOOD: Is a good idea to pick up it now, as you will need it for LESSON 5.

SCRAPS OF CLEAR GLASS: Go to your local auto and window glass dealer and ask them to sell you some scraps. Many times they will just give them to you. Tell them you want mostly single strength glass, but you would like a little double strength if they have some. It doesn't matter if it's slightly scratched or broken into odd shapes.

SAFETY GLASSES: If you wear prescription glasses, use those. Many department stores have clear "sunglasses" that are more comfortable and attractive than the hardware store glasses. Whatever you choose, wear glasses throughout the whole process.

X-ACTO KNIFE: A #1 size with extra #11 blades. Other brands are fine.

SCISSORS: For cutting paper.

CELLULOSE SPONGES: A package of four (medium size). These are the sponges that get hard when they dry out...not the big soft car sponges!

A SOFT BRISTLE, SHORT HANDLED BRUSH: For sweeping off your work area.

BAND-AIDS: No kidding! after a while you won't care about the cuts, but you'll want to keep the blood off your pattern.

LESSON 4

TRACING PAPER: A small tablet.

LESSON 5 - 6

STRIPS OF WOOD: Usually 1" x 2" strips will do but be sure they are straight. Trim wood is usually straight and works well if it is at least 3/4 inch wide on one end. (Don't use a hardwood such as oak, or you'll have to drill holes in it first!). You need pieces long enough to frame in three sides of PATTERN 1. In this case the window measures 8" x 10", so you need 1 strip about 10" long, and 2 strips about 12" long. Go to any lumber-yard.

NAILS: Long enough to go through your strips and into the plywood base without going all the way through to the other side. The nails should have heads on them (NOT finishing nails). Get a couple of hands full.

HORSESHOE NAILS: A small package from your supplier (about 20 should do).

CLAW HAMMER

THE BEST SQUARE YOU CAN FIND: This should be an "L" square, preferably metal.

A 12" METAL RULER: If it has metric on one side, it's worth paying extra for.

TWO ACCURATE COPIES OF PATTERN 1: With enough extra paper on all sides for taping down.

LESSON 7

GLASS: Choose your own glass according to the quantities printed on the pattern. NOTE: See "How to handle Glass" Ill 1-B.

LEAD CAME: Usually comes in 10 ft rolls. You need one roll of 3/16 H came.

LEAD VICE: I recommend one that has a *spring closure*.

COPPER FOIL: 7/32 is a good, medium width; one roll, 1.5 ml.

ZINC CAME: 3/16 outer bar, "U" shaped.

LEAD CUTTERS: These are a plier-type tool, not a knife.

WIRE CUTTERS: *Different* from lead cutters

GLASS GRINDER: I recommend a glass grinder as soon as you can get one. A sickle stone helps, but can't do the job that a glass grinder can do.

MORTON GRID: A very handy, inexpensive cutting surface that can also be used as a jig for cutting geometric shapes as you add accessories. Especially helpful if work space is limited.

FID*: For opening the lead channel

LESSON 8 - 9

FOILING PATTERN SHEARS: Not *lead* pattern shears. The *center* of the cutter is thinner for cutting out the thickness of the *foil*.

LESSON 10

SOLDERING IRON: An 80 watt wedge tip is a good beginners iron.

FLUX: Get two kinds: Paste and liquid.

FLUX BRUSH

SOLDERING STAND OR METAL ICE TRAY

SOLDER SYRINGE OR WICK*: For removing excess solder.

60/40 SOLDER: 60% tin and 40% lead.

WIRE BRUSH: A small (tooth-brush) size.

LESSON 11

GREY (DAP 33) PUTTY: Glazing compound.

PLASTER OF PARIS: A small carton.

NATURAL BRISTLE SCRUB BRUSH: These have bristles the color of light straw and are NOT plastic.

PAPER TOWELS

NAIL BRUSH: Just a cheap one.

PENCIL

PATINA: The color of your choice.

LESSON 12

LIGHT BOX*: Instructions for building one follow chapter 12

STAINED GLASS *DESIGN* SECRETS : You can design, even if you can't draw! This book will let you get the most out of your Stained Glass skills.

Have you got it all? Do you have a surface to work on? You need a flat, sturdy, hard surface on which to put your plywood. If the table is tall, so much the better (it's easier on your back). Cover your work surface with a double layer of the white paper. Your work surface should always have paper on it, and the paper should be CLEAN. Chips of glass on your paper can ruin your glass by scratching it or causing it to break when pressure is applied. If you use a Morton grid for cutting, you will eliminate some of the worry about small glass chips, as the grid "catches" the tiny chips and keeps them away from your glass. Even with a grid, you will still need the covered wood for cutting some small pieces. Cut a 1 in. square of the sponge and place it in the bottom of the jar. Saturate the sponge in the bottom of the jar with cutting oil, do not put enough cutting oil in the jar to cause a puddle. Put the cutting wheel end of your glass cutter on the saturated sponge and *leave* it there. The cutter should be placed on the oily sponge between each cut to keep the wheel lubricated.

ABOUT
CUTTING GLASS

F or most people, this is by far the most difficult part of stained glass production. It is best to go into this lesson expecting to get a few cuts , and somewhat frustrated. (There's that word again!) If you are honest with yourself about this, then you will see that it won't be long before your hands and eyes become accurate. Stick with it! Practice often. A half hour twice a day is better than two hours one day and none the next. If you do this for a week, you will be able to make 90% of the cuts you encounter in a panel. NOT BAD FOR A WEEK'S WORK!

SECRET: Tape your fingers with masking tape (not too tight) and between the pointer and second finger of your favored hand (See Illustration 1-A). Here's the pro tip: Now go wet and dry your hands.

The masking tape will quickly become as comfortable as a second skin. (The tape will try to come off if you have hand lotion on). You will avoid many blisters and cuts this way.

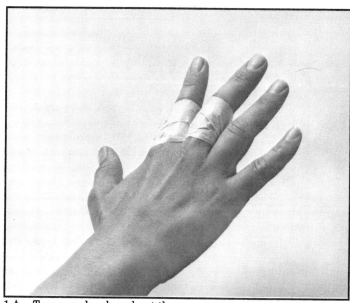

1-A.   Tape your hands and wet them

GLASS SAFETY

To handle glass safely, there are a few basic rules.

1. *Never* carry glass flat. It can break under its own weight.

2. Always carry glass with two hands, one hand under the glass and one on top. (If you can't reach top and bottom, then use bottom and front side, as high as your arm will reach.)

3. To lay a sheet of glass down, bring it up to the table in the vertical carrying position you carry it in. With the middle of the sheet touching the table edge, quickly tip the top edge down using the table as a support in the middle. Be sure you are supporting the lower edge and slide it *(without lifting it up!)* onto the table (See Illustration 1-B). Large or very flexible glass should have a person on each end.

4. Wear covered shoes, **not sandals!**

5. Treat glass with respect, *never* move too quickly or carelessly with it. Even a small piece can cause big injuries!

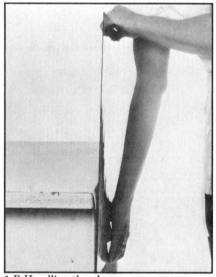

1-B Handling the glass.

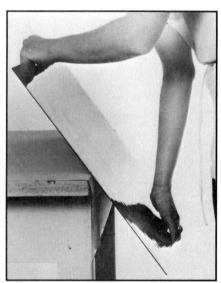

1-B

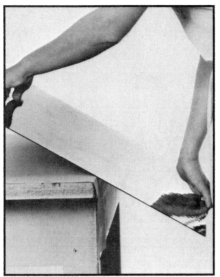
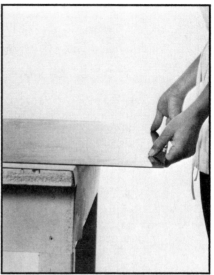

1-B Handling the glass.　　　　　　　　　　　　1-B

To successfully cut glass and avoid breaking it, you should understand how a glass cutter works. The wheel is pointed, and rolls freely when oiled. When rolled along the surface of glass, with pressure applied, it scratches the glass. This scratch is called a SCORE. Remember that word, it comes up often!

Although only the surface of the glass is scratched, the surface tension is released, and the density is disturbed through to the opposite side (See Illustration 1-C). What this means, is that a weak spot is created, that will allow the glass to break evenly along the score. It also means that you must hold the cutter vertical to the glass, not to one side. You also **cannot** score on the same line twice.

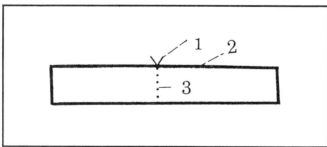

1-C 1) Cutting wheel 2) Edge of glass 3) Weakened glass

NOTE: If you do score on top of another score, that nice straight line of weakened glass will become a jumbled mess, and the glass will not break as well, if at all. You can also ruin your glass cutter, as the wheel will be chipped. Be sure you work with clean glass. Your cutter and score will be happier.

Put a piece of your scrap glass on the paper. Using your fine-tip pen, draw a straight line on the glass, leaving at least a half inch of glass on either side of the mark. Make a peace sign (remember those?) with your favored hand and place the end handle of the cutter on top of the "V".

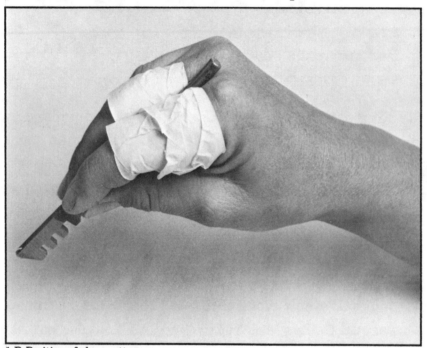

Put your pointer and second finger on top of the flat spot towards the cutting end of the cutter. The second finger may have to rest slightly to the side of the flat spot. Make sure the cutter is right side up (See Illustration 1-D).

1-D Position of glass cutter.

Now I know that you may be saying that you've seen cutters designed and used in different ways. Indulge me for just this week. If you learn to use this method of holding a cutter, your cuts will be smoother and more accurate. By having both fingers on top, you can move the cutter back and forth without twisting your wrist as you would with a pencil grip. After you are familiar with a traditional glass cutter, you can try the variations and make an informed decision on which cutter suits you best. Some of you may want to try a different grip for more pressure or better fit for your hand.

STAND UP! Press the cutting wheel down at the top edge of the glass on the black line. *YOU MUST START AT THE EDGE OF THE GLASS.* This rule never changes. Now, while applying a good amount of pressure, score the glass on the line by pulling the cutter towards you.

> **SECRET:**
>   A good score will sound like paper tearing.

Go ahead and tear a piece and see if you matched the sound. Chances are that you didn't. You may have pressed too hard, and the sound was grittier and rougher than the paper. Most likely you didn't press hard enough...no problem; you don't have to be King Kong to get a good score. The next paragraph is for you.

THE TRICK IS TO LEAN ON THE GLASS CUTTER, NOT TO PUSH (See Illustration 1-E).

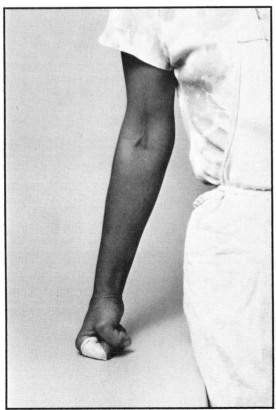

1-E Lean with braced arm.

> **SECRET:** Make a fist. STAND next to your work table and support yourself by leaning on the fingers of your fist. In order to do this, your wrist must be straight, and your muscles braced to make your elbow rigid. The pressure on your hand would be quite enough to get a good score.

Now try the straight line score again. This time concentrate on keeping your wrist from falling, and extend your elbow just far enough to "lean" on the glass. (See Illustration 1-F and 1-G).

REMINDER: Don't score on top of the other score!

> **SECRET:** This score is good sample to check for chips in your glass cutters wheel. (Of course it's not likely that you have any YET). Look at your score. If you see a "skip" in the score at very regular intervals, then your cutter is probably chipped. See illustration 1-H.

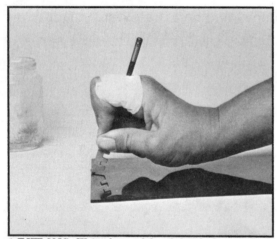

1-F WRONG: Wrist dropped, hand clenched, upper body relaxed.

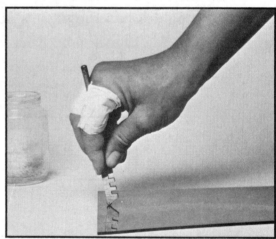

1-G RIGHT: Wrist up, pressure from upper body, arm braced.

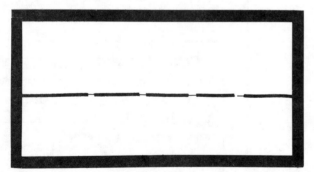

1-H A skip in the score means a chipped cutter.

> **SECRET:** To get a good "snap", your knuckles should roll apart.

It's time to break the glass on the score. Hold the glass with your thumbs together, and the score between them. Your knuckles should touch underneath the glass. Now snap the glass apart. Try this without glass...Put your knuckles together with both hands in a fist. Now roll them apart, starting with the top knuckle. When the small knuckle touches, the hands will break apart (See Illustration 1-I)

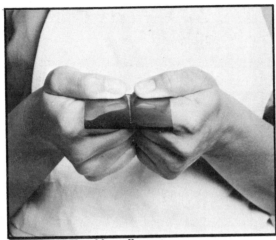

1-I. RIGHT Knuckles roll apart.

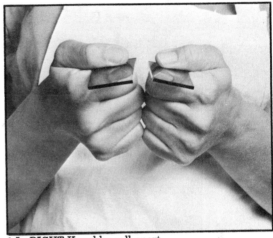

1-I. RIGHT Knuckles roll apart.

Practice this exercise until it feels natural. Even a good score won't break well if you don't snap it off correctly. A common mistake is to try to pull the glass apart, to push one side down or to hold the glass too far from the score. (See Illustration 1-J).With narrow pieces of glass, you need to use your grozers to pull the smallest piece away.

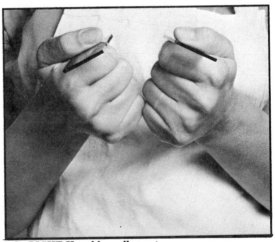

1-I. RIGHT Knuckles roll apart.

Eventually, you may need to buy two pairs of grozers to use when both sides are small. When using pliers, position the pliers as close to the to the score as possible without actually touching it and use your fist immediately opposite it. (See Illustration 1-K). If you place the pliers and fist too far from the score, the glass is stressed and may not have a clean snap. (See Illustration 1-L).

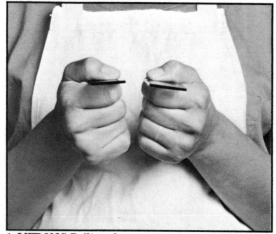

1-J WRONG Pulling glass apart.

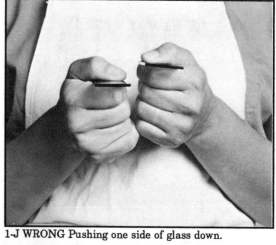

1-J WRONG Pushing one side of glass down.

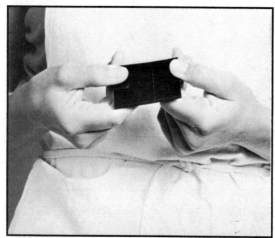

1-J WRONG Holding too far from the score.

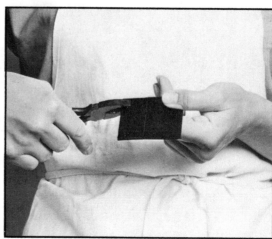

1-L WRONG Too far from the score.

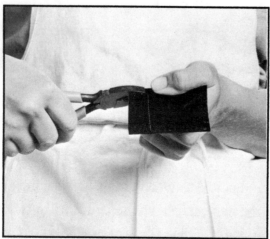

1-K RIGHT The fist and pliers roll apart from each other.

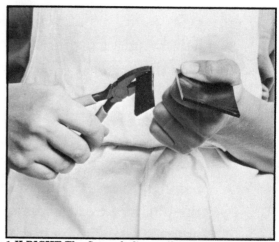

1-K RIGHT The fist and pliers roll apart.

It is very important not to crush the glass.

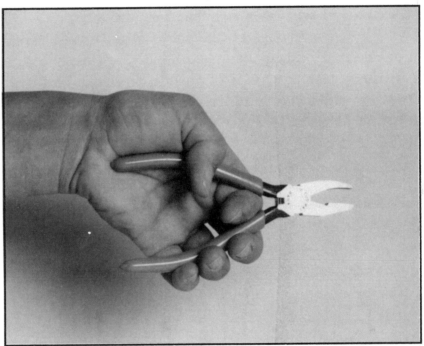

1-M Hold the pliers with your index finger between the handles.

The timing of breaking the score is important. The score will "heal" if not broken quickly. The glass is still scratched on the surface, but is not weakened all the way through to the other side. A score gets old after about two minutes, and is often referred to as "cold". So you can see that it is important to finish scoring and breaking all the shapes in your panels with efficient timing. Many professionals prefer to score several times before beginning to break the scores. This is a good habit to establish, as you will find you have smooth lines and continuity within each piece if you aren't stopping to change tools after each score.

LESSON TWO:
CUTTING SHAPES;
OUTSIDE CURVES

The first shape we will cut is an OUTSIDE CURVE. In other words, a circle. I will refer to outside curves anytime we are cutting portions of circles where the glass on the INSIDE of the circle remains intact. Are you remembering to keep the cutter oiled? Take the lid off your jar and place it in the corner of a piece of glass with about half inch outside edges. Trace around the edge of the lid with your felt tip pen. Cut the glass down to a workable size, leaving about a half inch of glass on all four sides. (See Illustration 2-A)

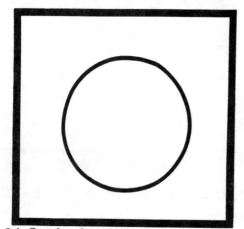

2-A Cut the glass down to a workable size, leaving at least a half inch on each side.

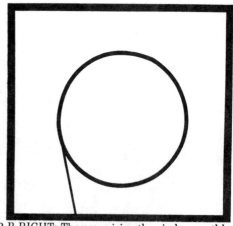

2-B RIGHT: The score joins the circle smoothly.

With your cutter starting at the edge of the glass *(always)*, score into the circle (See Illustration 2-B). Notice that the score joins the circle without having to turn a corner.

TIP: Glass tends to break in a straight line! If you keep this in mind, you can plan your cuts where they are most likely to break cleanly.
Try to score the circle with one score by turning the glass as you cut. If **you**

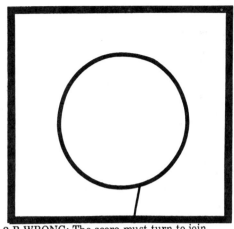

2-B WRONG: The score must turn to join.

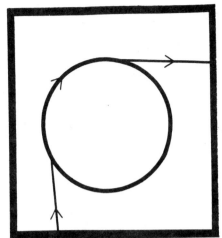

2-C RIGHT: Scoring off the glass in as straight a line as possible.

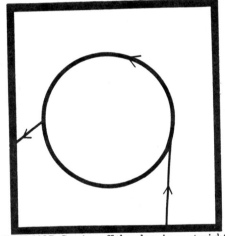

2-C WRONG: Scoring off the glass in as straight a line as possible.

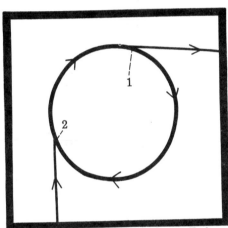

2-D Finishing the score: 1. Begin 2. End

cannot complete the circle, score off the glass the same way you started:

DON'T TURN ANY SHARP CORNERS!!! (See Illustration 2-C). To complete the circle, slide your cutter along the glass until you feel it meet the score at the exact place that you left the circle.

DO NOT SCORE OVER THE OLD SCORE. Now complete the circle, stopping when you get to the beginning of the score. (Believe me, you'll hear it if you score on top of a score!) It is not necessary to score off the glass (See Illustration 2-D).

Time out for problem solving. Is your score on the black line...anywhere? If it is, GREAT. If not, does it look like this? (See Illustration 2-E).

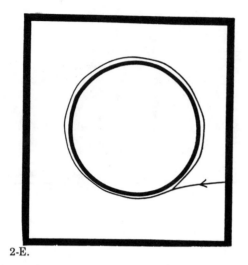

2-E.

SECRET: If your score is following an almost even path on either side of the black line, it's because you are looking at the cutter instead of the line it's supposed to be following.

If you are on again off again scoring, you may be looking back and forth from the cutter to the line. In both cases, you will benefit from the next secret.

SECRET: Force your eyes to look at the line about an inch or so in front of your cutter. As you practice this, your hand will learn to follow your line of vision and your cuts will be accurate.

To demonstrate this point, imagine what would happen if you looked at the front end of your car while driving instead of the road in front of it!

OK, back to the circle.

The score that forms the circle is called the PRIMARY score. The circle itself is the PRIMARY PIECE (it is the piece you want to keep). Any and all cuts that are not part of the shape itself are called SECONDARY scores. Secondary scores are there to help the shape break out of the BACKGROUND GLASS. They provide the "straight" lines for breaking.

This circle needs some more secondary scores. Begin these scores by sliding the cutter into the primary score until you feel them meet, and then scoring off to the edge of the glass. The first secondary score that you add should line up with the secondary score that is already there (See Illustration 2-F).

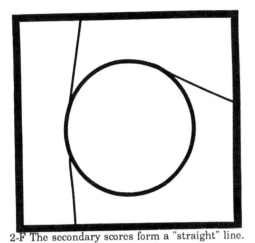

2-F The secondary scores form a "straight" line.

The rest of the secondary scores come off in tangents from the circle, and do not have to line up. (See Illustration 2-G).

This is always the first score to break off (See Illustration 2-G).

Break this score off, using your pliers to hold one side of the glass. Make sure that the pliers are right side up. The arch side of the pliers should be up. Your other hand is in the *fist position.*

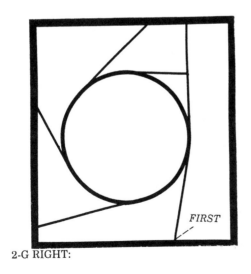

FIRST

2-G RIGHT:

Both fist and pliers are close to the score, near the edge of the glass. The pliers and fist should break apart with the same

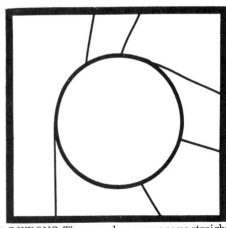

2-G WRONG: The secondary scores come straight off the circle.

rolling motion as the two fists had in **Illustration 1-I.**

Do not crush your glass by holding the pliers too tightly.

Break off the remaining secondary scores the same way, always breaking off one that leads to the previous break (See Illustration 2-H).

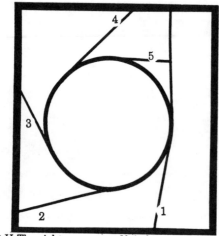

2-H The right sequence of breaks.

There will be points of glass left, which should be removed with careful use of the pliers. This is a great exercise for learning to properly use the grozing pliers. Too much pressure will definitely not work on these tiny pieces of glass! If the small pieces slant towards the back side of the glass, you may have to turn the glass over to get a good grip on them.

Practice these outside curves until you have three good circles.

LESSON THREE: INSIDE CURVES

By this time, you should be comfortable with basic scoring, and outside curves are not too big of a problem. If this is not true, practice some more before going on to this lesson.

Place a piece of glass on the CLEAN work surface. Place the jar lid at the bottom of the glass so that it forms a half circle (See Illustration 3-A). Be sure you have at least a half inch on either side of the half circle.

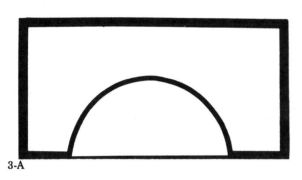

3-A

You are going to remove the inside of the half circle, leaving the outside intact. This is called an INSIDE CURVE, otherwise known as mouse-holes! The straight line rules apply to this cut, but are applied differently.

First, score the primary score (on the half circle line.) It is important that you do this with ONE score. Now score a shallow half circle from **point** to **point** of the Primary Score (See Illustration 3-B).

SECRET: With an inside curve, every secondary score MUST end on a previous Secondary Score, or the end of the glass) NOT ON THE PRIMARY SCORE! (Ill. 3-C)

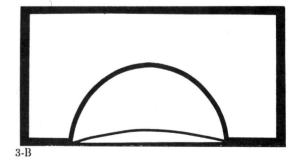

3-B

All of the other Secondary Scores are also shallow half circles, but may be shorter than the first.

The last secondary score is the one closest to the primary score (are you getting used to this vocabulary yet?). This score should "shadow" the primary score, NEVER touching it (See Illustration 3-D). Snap the secondary scores out of the glass using your pliers. Always keep your free hand in the fist position, opposite the pliers.
This puts much less stress on the glass, so that the shape doesn't break (See Illustration 3-E).

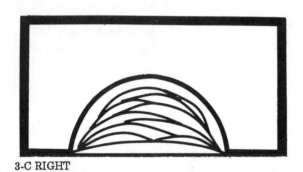

3-C RIGHT

3-C WRONG: Note that the shape may break dots by ending on the Primary Score!

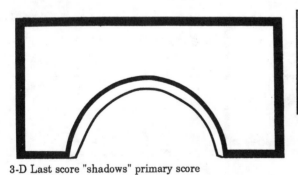

3-D Last score "shadows" primary score

SECRET: Gently flexing the glass will cause a run on a good score, giving you an advantage on very difficult cuts.

Breaking the glass from the end will allow the score to "run". A score runs when you can see the fracture through the glass before it actually breaks off. To flex the glass, put your hands or pliers in the position for breaking, and gently bend the glass. You can flex the glass with your fingers and pliers, or with a Morton running tool. Running pliers are useful for straight lines, but not reliable for shapes. If you use the pliers to flex the glass from both ends of the score, you can run the score around almost impossible cuts. If you are using the Morton running tool, flexing from the center of the most difficult (deepest) point and then following the run to the ends will make a very clean break. After the run has begun, you can help it along by pressing on the score just behind the run. The run will stay right in front of your fingers. Practice this, and it will make a huge difference in your success rate.

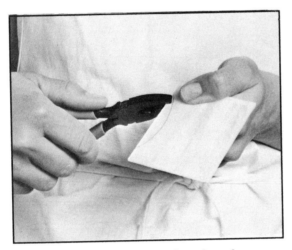

3-E RIGHT: Breaking the scores from the end.

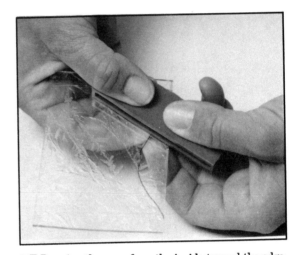

3-E Running the score from the inside toward the edge. (Using a Morton running tool.)

SECRET: The pliers should break the glass from the END of the score, NOT THE MIDDLE. The opposite is true if you are *running* the score first using a Morton running tool. To run the score you would run it from the center to the ends, then break out with the pliers at the end.

Let's talk a minute about tapping the glass to break it. First of all, tapping the glass with the end of your cutter can cause it to break on the score; second, it can also cause the a run to leave the score. Because the vibrations of the tapping travel throughout the glass, it is difficult to control the run. This method IS good for removing broken pieces from a finished, foiled panel, as the piece must be broken to be removed.

LESSON FOUR:
THE STRATEGY OF CUTTING

A COPY of the two patterns in this lesson (if your white paper isn't too dense, just trace them with that). Use the medium black felt tip pen.

ALL RIGHT!!! This is the lesson that pays for the book! Dog-ear the corner of this page and plan to use these example cuts as reference for your entire first or next window.

All cuts are made up of *inside curves*, *outside curves*, or *straight lines*, or a combination thereof. When you learn to break each cut down to it's components, the best cutting strategy will follow. Lets look at the two sample windows at the back of the book and approach some shapes individually. To simplify the explanations, I have placed each pattern piece on glass that is square or rectangle. I realize that your pieces may be different shapes, but the basic principals will still apply as long as you have at least a half inch of glass on all sides of the Primary piece.

I have numbered the cuts according to the order in which I cut them. "P" signifies that the score is on the PRIMARY line. The thinnest lines are SECONDARY scores. For clarity, I have enlarged the small pattern pieces. An explanation of the cuts follows each diagram. As your scores and breaks become more consistent, you may want to eliminate some of the Secondary Scores. It's my opinion, however, that you should give the glass every opportunity to break off clean and easy. Begin with illustration 4-A. Trace the piece on to the glass using the fine point pen. The pattern is positioned so that the INSIDE CURVE is closest to the edge. Inside curves tend to be the most difficult, and are usually cut first. There are two reasons for this. The first is that the pattern piece could be moved back onto unscored glass if the difficult cut breaks poorly.

The second reason seems obvious, but is one of the most overlooked principals in cutting:

SECRET: Leave as much glass as possible on the back side of an inside curve, it gives the piece strength which may be crucial in keeping the primary piece from breaking with the stress of your cuts. GOT IT? Good.

SCORE 1P brings the score from one edge of the glass, picks up the primary score (that's what the "P" is for) and continues to the other end of the glass (Avoid falling off the edge of the glass, it's hard on the cutter).

SCORE 2 is "point to point" of the inside curve.

SCORE 3 is a shallow half moon that leaves a "shadow" under the primary score.

SECRET: Use your pliers starting at the "pointed end" of the piece, not the middle. Even if the score is bad, this allows the thin piece of background glass to break and is less likely to break the primary piece.

Break off these scores now (2 then 3 then 1P) using your pliers on the background glass and your hand opposite it.

SCORE 4P begins where SCORE 1 left the primary piece and travels off the glass when it reaches the sharp corner on the left side. This continuous cut is

SECRET: NEVER, NEVER, NEVER score ANYTHING you can't see. Keep the glass positioned so the ink line is between you and the cutter.

best achieved by turning the glass on the paper.
4-B SCORE 5, 6, 7, and 8 respectively, and break off in the same sequence (See Illustration 4-B. Note that SCORE 5 doesn't need another score to line up with it, because it ends at the *edge* of the glass. (See lesson #2, illustration 2- G.)

4-C Score 9, To lessen the strength of the background glass. Break off last piece.

Clean-up the little chunks of glass and remember to practice gently

using your grozers. If you get chips shaped like half-moons, it's from too much pressure.

These "Perfect-Bite" pliers arch on both sides, so there is no "wrong side-up"!

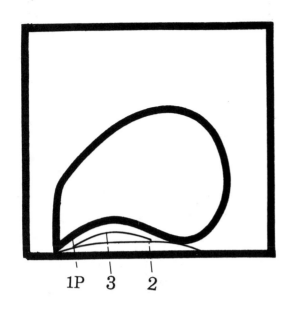

1P   3   2

4-A PIECE 1 from pattern 1

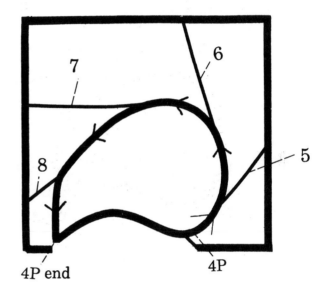

7   6

8

5

4P end   4P

4-B

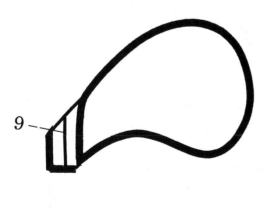

9

4-C

Use illustration 4-D. This is a tough one. When two inside curves come together to form a point, the point is always vulnerable. Of course, ANY point has a possibility of breaking, and the thinner the point, the weaker it is.

PAY ATTENTION!! This part is important: Wouldn't you rather break the background than the primary piece?

> **SECRET:** Never pull a very large piece of glass off of a small point. The smaller piece is weaker and more likely to break.

SCORE 1P, and 2. (Note the shadow effect.) Break off 2, 1.

SCORE 3 and break off, with your fist under the side towards the primary side, and your grozers next to the score on the background side. Remember to have your thumb right next to the score, and the pliers right across from your thumb.

4-E: SCORE 4 is a "Chicken Score". Use it if you aren't really confident with the other scores (or if this is your second try with this part). Break off 4 using the same method as SCORE 3. Even after you are experienced with glass it is a good idea to use "Chicken Scores" if the cut is difficult or the glass is hard to work with. SCORE 5 and break off.

SCORE 6P, and 7. Break off 7, 6P, Be sure your fist is supporting the primary piece right next to the score, especially at the point during the breaks! Remember to position the pliers at the pointed end of the background glass when you begin your break, then you can work your way across if it decides to break off in pieces.

QUIZ TIME: Do you see why SCORE 4 was scored and broken before 5, 6, and 7?   This was to keep from breaking a large piece off the point. I didn't score and break SCORE 4 before 1, 2, and 3 so that the background could add extra strength.

Both of the large inside curves are now cut. It's time to cut the other side, which is a combination of outside and inside curves, again coming together at a point.

The strategy that we will use is to first reduce the background glass on the side that we are cutting, score the primary piece, then use secondary scores to break the outside curve, and finish by breaking the inside curve (See Illustration 4-F).

SCORE 1 and break off. Now there's less glass to "pull" against the primary

---

SECRET: With cuts like this, always break the glass so that the break *starts with the primary score* and *ends with the secondary score*. The closer your hands are to the break, the more control you have over how it breaks. Keep your hands and pliers close to the Primary Piece.

---

piece, making the primary piece relatively stronger.

SCORE 2 just to get a little closer. Break off.

SCORE 3P to the end of the primary score.

SCORE 4 from the primary score to the end of the glass. Break off, using pliers next to the 3P end.

Break off the remainder of P3. (Where are your pliers positioned?)

4-G: SCORE 5P. Score and break 6 then 7. Score 8 from the primary score to the glass edge. Break off last pieces.

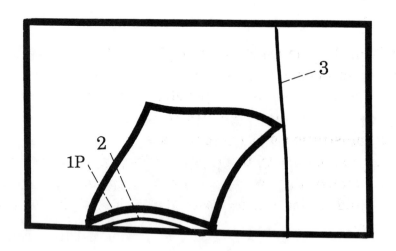

4-D PIECE 2, pattern 1

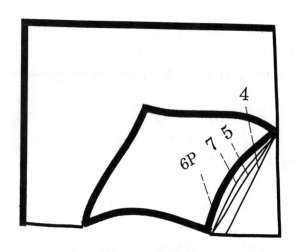

4-E

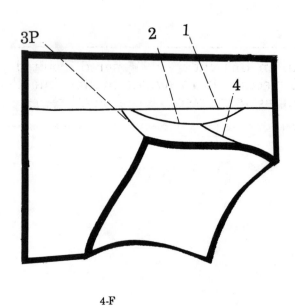

4-F

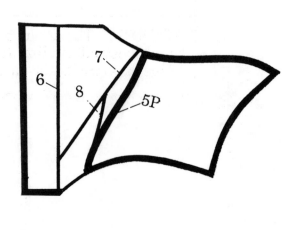

4-G

34

Let's move on to pattern 2. These pieces are typical of long tapers and thin curves. It is important to master this type of cut if you want to maintain graceful lines in your designs. While it is possible to add break lines and simplify the cut, the designs are never as smooth with extra lead lines that can be avoided. Trace illustration 4-H on your glass.

SCORE 1 is one of the exceptions to the rule of scoring point-to-point on an inside curve. This is because the two points are already on the edge of the glass, and the glass would be too narrow to easily work with if the scores were any closer together.

SCORE 2P and break off 1, then 2. One more time...*use your pliers starting at the pointed end and work your way across.* 4-H

Trace the secondary scores from illustration 4-I on your glass.
SCORE 3P, 4 and 5P and break off in the same order. The primary piece is getting thin, so it important to support it with your fist as you use the pliers opposite it.
4-J : With the cuts we have made, the piece looks like this. SCORE 1 and break off. This brings the size of the background glass down to a less threatening size, yet leaves it big enough to work with.

SCORE 2 and break off (which end are you breaking from and supporting?)

SCORE 3 and 4P and break off 3 and 4P. Whew! If you got that one give yourself a pat on the back!

SECRET: The main principal on this cut was : Tapered, pointed pieces break best off of slim, tapered pieces. It's a tongue twister, but it's true. This is a variation on not pulling large pieces off of small pieces.

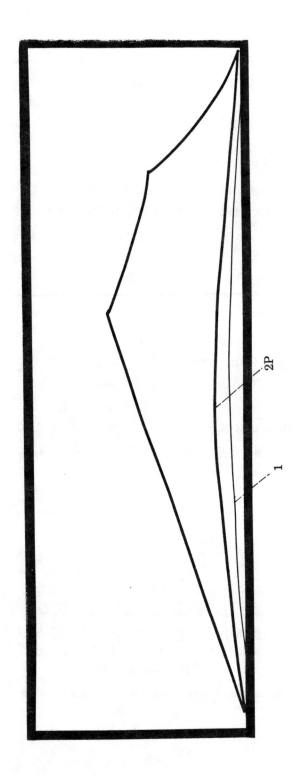

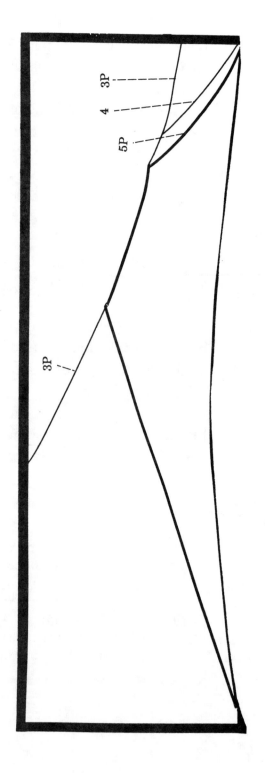

4- H PIECE 1, pattern 2

4-I

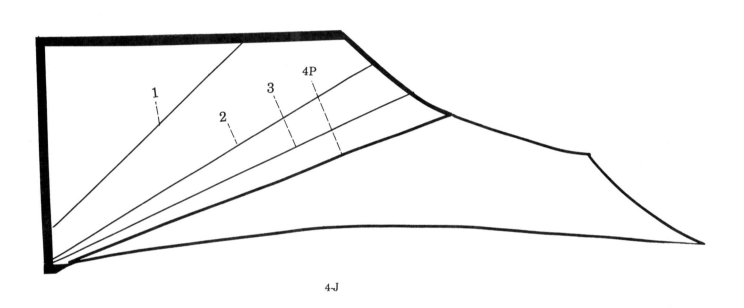

4-J

Trace illustration 4-K. Place the pattern so that the ends do not touch the edge of the glass. Do you see why? If you brought the pattern down any lower, there wouldn't be enough glass to break off of 4P and 5P easily.

SCORE 1 is point-to-point. Break off.

SCORE 2 brings it in a little closer. Break off. This shape is so shallow, that you probably don't need more secondary scores.

SCORE 3P and break off.

4-L: SCORE 4P and 5P and break off. **Support that Primary Piece!**

SCORE 6 and break off.

Trace the secondary scores from illustration 4-M.

SCORE 1 and 2 to eliminate excess glass. Break off.

SCORE 3 and 4 Ditto.

SCORE 5P and 6. Break off 5P, with the score running off score 6. Break off the rest of 5P. The primary piece will need lots of support.

That's it! If you got one of each of the pieces cut, "you done good"! Let's learn how to build a window.

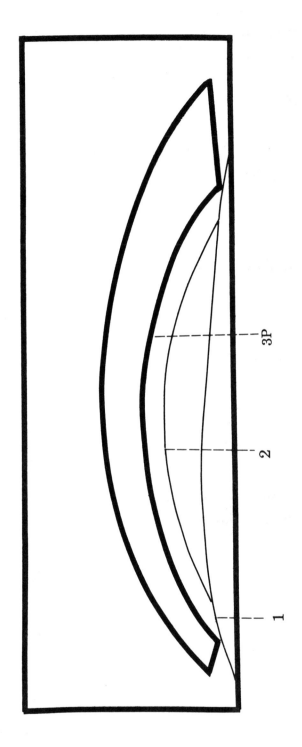

4-K PIECE 2, pattern 2

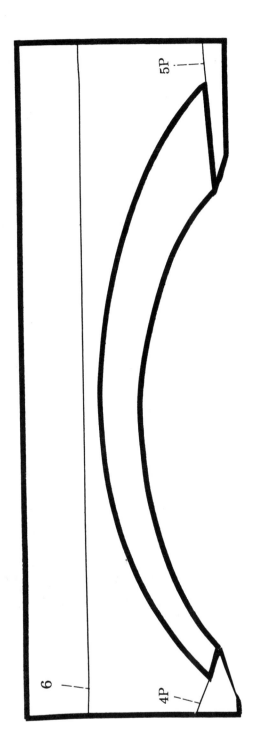

4-L

39

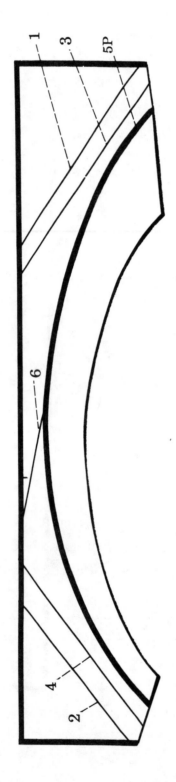

4-M

LESSON FIVE:
HOW TO SET UP A WINDOW

C over one of your plywood sheets with white paper, and place a copy of Pattern 1 in the lower left corner of the board. Tape the pattern down.

Hammer 3 nails into each of the wood strips (middle and toward each end).

SECRET: Once the wood is positioned, you will have a much better chance of keeping it in place if the nails are ready to connect the wood.

Hammer them almost all the way through, but not quite.
Place one of the 10" strips against the bottom line of your pattern. Hammer in the nails.

TIP: Ok, some of you know this, but most women I've taught didn't. Hold the hammer down on the lower part of the handle. You can more clearly see what you are aiming at (so you're less likely to hit your thumb!) and you'll have more leverage. It only seems more secure to hold the hammer closer to the head.

Place the L-square against this piece of wood and line up the "L" corner with the left hand side of the corner. Place a piece of 10" wood on the board, against the bottom of the square (See Illustration 5-A).

When you have the strip flush with the square, hammer in the nails. The third strip of wood is going on the right side, opposite the one you just put on. This strip will not be measured in place with the square (even if your square fits inside the frame!). The most accurate way to measure a parallel line is straight across from the other side. Does this sound like geometry class? Using your ruler, measure across 8" from the left strip. Do this in at least three places (See Illustration 5-B). Mark the 8" point with a "V", not a dot. Yea, Yea, there is at least one cabinet maker out there saying "I knew that." So...who do you think told me?

SECRET: Dots are not as easy to accurately line up with as "V"'s are. Remember this and use it every time you mark a measurement on glass or anywhere else. You will make far less errors!

5-A Beginning to board up a window.

All flat-sided windows can be laid out and boarded up in this way. There are products on the market that are meant to replace the wood strips and plywood. These have some use on small projects, but I haven't seen any that are as versatile as old fashioned wood.

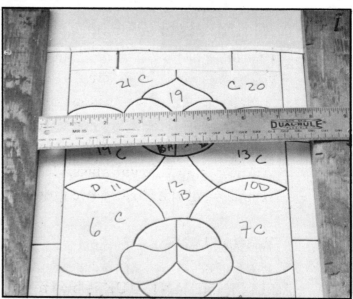

5-B Measuring across for accuracy.

LESSON SIX: ABOUT THE WINDOW'S MATERIALS.

It's time to get the glass for your first window. First, it helps if you have an idea of what you're looking at when you go to your supplier. This lesson is a general overview of Stained Glass.

There are three basic types of Stained Glass:

ANTIQUE

While this glass isn't actually old, it is made very much like the glass was made centuries ago. It is usually transparent, and catches the light very well. It is made by "hand" by glass blowers, and is often of varying widths because of this. It tends to scratch more than most glass. You will also hear people refer to Antique as "Blown" glass. It usually cuts very well. Antique is the most expensive of the three basic types.

VARIATIONS:

MACHINE ANTIQUE is blown with the aid of machines, and is considerably less expensive. The brilliance is still good, though a skilled eye can tell the difference. It is more regular in width, and the surface stress lines are also regular.

CRAQUEL is Blown glass with a texture resembling alligator skin. The texture is sharp and must be handled with care. See the cleaning lesson on how to handle this lovely glass. Cut on the smooth side.

FLASHED may appear to be a different color than it really is! It is actually a layer of glass with a thinner layer "flashed" on top of it. While the Antique was being blown, it was dipped into a vat of another color just before it was cut open and laid flat. The colors are wonderful, and when you learn to etch you will appreciate the possibilities in removing areas of the color. Cut on the main color.

SEEDY means air bubbles. They're not mistakes.

REAMY looks like someone stretched the molten glass with their fingers. It adds great motion and texture.

CATHEDRAL

Cathedral glass is also usually transparent, though it doesn't catch the light as well or have the brilliance of antique. It is machine rolled glass; literally rolled out on tables by machine. The cutting quality of Cathedral glass varies with the manufacturer. It is very regular in width. There are a multitude of textures, since the glass takes on whatever texture the table had. Some different types of Cathedral glass are:

STREAKY is just like it sounds: there are transparent streaks of color throughout the glass.

WISPY is very lightly streaked.

IRIDESCENT has a thin film of iridescence on (usually) one side. Some brands require cutting on the non-iridescent side.

SEEDY air bubbles. See Antique.

GLUE CHIP looks like Jack Frost crystals! It comes in a variety of colors, though clear is by far the most common. Cut on smooth side.

OPAL OR OPALESCENT

Any glass that has a milky quality, or cannot be easily seen through in any

OPAL OR OPALESCENT

area. The most easily recognizable Opal is completely opaque; this is the glass most of us relate to traditional windows and Tiffany style lamps. Streaky Opals and Streaky Cathedrals can easily be confused, and only the manufacturer seems to know for sure! Like Cathedral, this glass is rolled. The only time I have seen an exception to this is when Antique is Flashed with Opal. Opal is usually more difficult to cut than other glass, though manufacturers, in recent years, have made great strides in this area.

STREAKY means streaks of non-transparent color; the glass is considered Opal even if the background is somewhat transparent.

WISPY means very lightly streaked.

CATS PAW is a mottling of the color that resembles paw prints.

OTHER GLASS

Other glass that you'll want to become familiar with include: beveled glass, jewels, glass globs, rondelles, and novelty glass such as **dichroic** The stained glass manufacturers are very creative in their art, and new glass is coming out every day. The best way to keep abreast of the state-of-art stained glass is to find a good supplier that will take the time to communicate with you. This is a relationship worth developing!

LEAD CAME

Lead Came comes in long strips, and a variety of widths and shapes. "C" or"U" shapes have a channel on one side and are for outer edges of projects. "H" shape has two channels for holding two pieces of glass together.

SOLDER

Solder is usually lead and tin. It is usually referred to by the content of each of these metals. 50-50 is 50% tin and 50% lead, 60-40 is 60% tin and 40% lead. The higher the tin content, the wider the range that the solder will flow without being dull and pasty, and so it is easier to work with. (Unfortunately it is also more expensive). Solder will bond to certain metals ONLY, such as copper, lead, tin and some steel.

FLUX

Flux is a is a paste or liquid that is applied to the metal before soldering to chemically clean it. It removes oxidants so that the solder can bond and flow well.

COPPER FOIL

Copper foil is a copper tape that is wrapped around the glass edges to give the solder a surface to adhere to.

PATINA

Patina is a chemical that oxidizes the solder and darkens it quickly. It comes in a variety of finishes for different effects.

LESSON SEVEN: BUILDING A WINDOW WITH A LEAD BORDER

I've chosen a project for your first window which can be built with both lead and copper foil. While you may develop a preference for one or the other techniques, it is of a GREAT advantage to be able to do both. For this window the border will be leaded and the interior will be foiled. The outside edge will be zinc.

This lesson requires spending more money and accumulating more tools than any of the others. Cheer up--Most of the tools will last you for years; and the solder and foil will last for the first few projects too. There's no doubt that Stained Glass is one of the more expensive art forms, and that it's well worth it! If you haven't already done so, this is the time to get a good, professional quality glass cutter (and throw the cheap one away). Stained glass is too valuable to risk using a poor quality cutter!!!

Since we will be working with stained glass for the first time, there are a few cutting characteristics to be aware of. Some HIGH COLOR Antique glass has a silent score; and some have a dull side that doesn't score well. (Score on shiny side) Most Opal glass has to be scored harder to get a good break; some will score silently. Always score on the smoothest side of any glass.
Once again, be sure the glass is clean!

To begin, mount your lead vice on a secure wall, preferably screwing into a stud. Be sure the vice is well anchored, because even a little bit of slack can be a problem. There should be a clear aisle in front of the vice of at least 5 ft Cut your lead into two 5 ft pieces, bend one end over about an inch and hang them from anything tall enough to keep them off the floor. An open door works well. Take them one at a time and place one end in the vice with the channel facing sideways (See Illustration 7-A). There should be at least a couple of inches in the vice.

Now run your fingers down the channels to keep the lead from twisting until you are holding the other end and standing back as far as you can from the vice. Hold the end with the pliers, again with the channel sideways in the

SECRET: Always place one foot behind you in a shoulder width stance before you pull back. This will help keep you from landing on your bottom if the lead should break or come out of the vice.

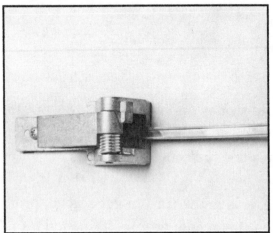

7-A The lead in the vice, channel to side.

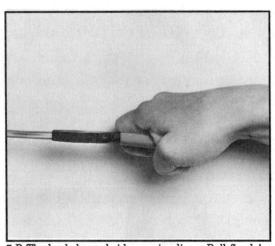

7-B The lead channel sideways in pliers. Pull firmly!

pliers (See Illustration 7-B). Keeping a firm grip on the pliers pull gently and firmly back until you see the lead straighten.

Release the lead from the vice, and let that end fall. Bend the other end over about 2 in. and hang back up.

Just a word of CAUTION about working with lead and solder (Which is about half lead). Please don't take *any* chances of getting either of these in your mouth. Lead poisoning is very dangerous and simple precautions are all it takes to avoid it. The lead does NOT enter your blood through your skin, it must be ingested.

Make it a rule not to eat or drink while working with either solder or lead. Keep your hands away from your face. If you are pregnant you should consult your doctor about the risks. As long as we're on the subject of safety, are you still wearing your glasses?

Now you have two nice, straight pieces of lead hanging up. Let's work with the zinc. Keep the zinc flat and straight as you work with it. It is hard to straighten after it's bent. We are working with U shaped zinc, which is relatively thin, so it can be cut with sharp wire-cutters. Wire cutters look a lot like lead cutters, but they cannot be used interchangeably. Remember the straight, flush side of the lead cutters? Notice that the wire cutters are beveled

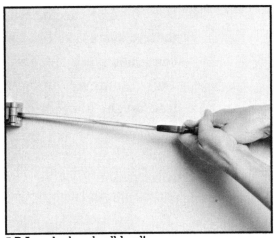

7-B Lean back and pull hard!

on both sides, so they don't cut the straight edge you need on lead. If you use the lead cutters on zinc, wire or other hard metals, the blade may chip! If the zinc were thicker we would have to cut it with a hack-saw.

Measure down 8 inches from the top and mark. (Remember to use a "V" for accuracy) Use your thin felt tip to mark a 90 degree angle at that spot. Cut the zinc straight across. Place the zinc in the bottom of the wood frame with the channel facing toward the pattern. Cut two more pieces of zinc to fit against this piece and end at the top of your pattern. Place these in the wood frame also (See Illustration 7-C).

Now let's cut the glass for the border. Insert your metal ruler in the zinc and measure to the *inside* of the black line. Notice that this line is thicker than theinternal design. This is to allow room for the lead core. We are avoiding having to buy special scissors called LEAD PATTERN SHEARS by measuring to where the glass sits in the lead. You may want to buy a pair of these shears if you decide to lead a whole project (they cut a channel out of the pattern to allow for the lead).

SECRET: If your metal ruler has metric lines on one side, use those lines. The metric lines are closer together and allow you to be more accurate. Part B of this secret is to mark the measurement on the ruler. This way you don't have to find it each time and there is less chance that you'll misread the measurement.

For the most accuracy, USE METRIC !! You don't have to understand the metric system to take advantage of the smaller lines!. Then when you measure the glass place the #1 mark on the edge of the glass, not the end of the ruler. This allows you to sight down the rule and the glass edge instead of trying to line up the glass and the end of the ruler.

Don't forget to compensate for this at the end of your measurement! (See Illustration 7-D).

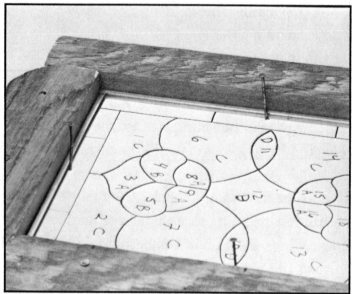

7-C The Zinc is held in by nails.

7-D Measuring accurately from inside the ruler

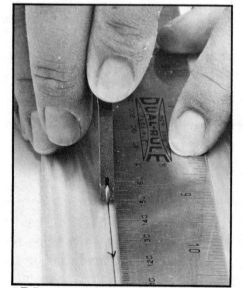

7-F Compensate for the cutters width, ruler is not on line.

First, decide which direction you want the streaks of the Opal glass to run and keep it consistent.

SECRET: To really increase your accuracy, move the measurement over on the ruler by one inch (or one centimeter). ie: If you marked 1.5 change it to 2.5.

7-D Straight lines break off easily by running the score with a Morton "button".

With the #1 on the edge of the glass, measure over to the marked line and mark the glass in at least three places.

> **SECRET:** In life, two points determine a straight line. In Glass, it takes at least three points to determine a line. Yes, they lied to you in geometry class!

Why? Because of what I call the rule of multiplied error, instead of being parallel, the two lines begin to form a triangle!

ie: If one of your points "V"s is 1/16th of an inch off (which is not much) and you line your straight edge up with it, then the top of the straight edge will be about 1/4 of an inch off after only 12 inches (that's a lot!).

Now lets cut the glass on the marked line. To line the ruler up on the points,

> **SECRET:** Tape pennies to the back of your ruler with masking tape, and they will hold the edge up so the cutter doesn't catch on it. The masking tape will also make the metal rule less slippery on the glass.

place the cutters wheel exactly on the measured "V" and put the ruler snugly up against it. Do this on all "V"s and re-check each "V" before cutting. The cutter's width will bring the cut out about 1/16", which must be allowed for (See Illustration 7-F). Hold the ruler firmly against the glass. Pull the cutter straight back towards you, leaning down, and listen for a clean score.

If you wanted to make many of these straight pieces, then you could build a jig (See Illustration 7-G). (For those of you that have a cutting grid, ask your supplier for the accessories for strip cutting.) When you have some long border pieces cut, measure the length of the lower left hand corner, piece 5 (bottom) piece and cut. Remember to allow for the lead. Place this piece in the corner, in the zinc channel. Using the **flush** side of your lead cutters, cut a piece of lead about 6 ft long at a square angle. To keep from closing up the lead channel you will need to always cut *across* the lead, **not** up and down (See Illustration 7-H).

Place the lead against the zinc snugly, with the glass in the channel (See Illustration 7-I). If the lead channel is too narrow for the glass, you can use a FID to open the channel.

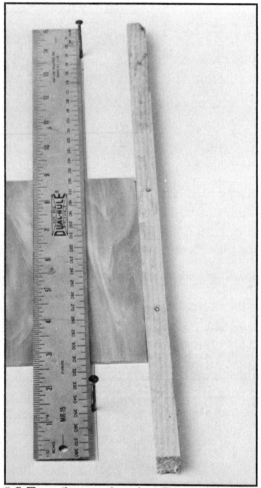

7-G The nails stops the ruler. The wood stops the glass.

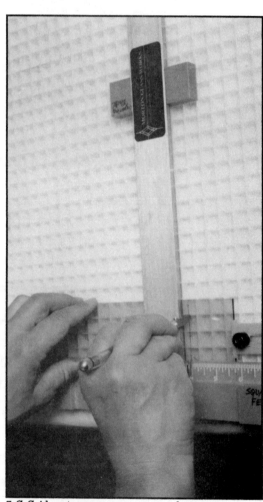

7-G Grid systems are very easy and accurate.

Now you must think ahead as to how the other pieces of lead will lay. We are going to put one long strip of lead across the top of these border pieces, so you need to leave room on the glass for the lead to cross. To do this, cut another strip of lead about 1" long (again squared), and place it on the top edge of the glass. The place where the two pieces of lead come together will tell you where to cut the first piece of lead (See Illustration 7-I).

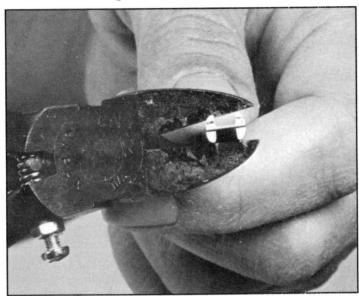

7-H RIGHT

Save this 1" piece of lead to use as a guide with the other lead. Mark the lead with your fine tip marker and cut with the lead cutters. Remember to cut *across* the channel, not up and down! The lead should meet snugly, (these meeting points are called "lead joints") or you may have soldering problems

later. One at a time, measure, cut and lead three sides of the border. When the long strips are in place, hold securely with nails against the lead. Some artists prefer to use flat horse-shoe nails for this. Pieces that are not ready yet for the long strips of lead can be held with scraps (See Illustration 7-J).

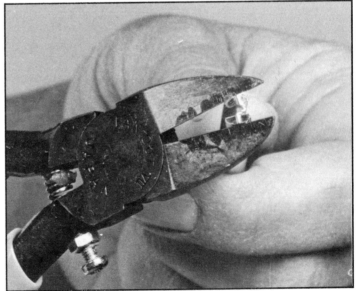

7-H WRONG

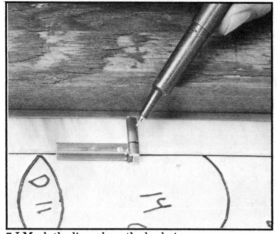
7-I Mark the line where the lead pieces cross

Though you are not going to lead the inside of this window, there are a few things you may need to know about leading curved lines. The space that the lead is cut back can be determined by using scraps, like we did in the border. The angle that the lead is cut is **very important** to the flow of the design (See Illustration 7-K). Remember that it is the shape of the lead that will show a good or poor line.

Different lead shapes can change the effect of the design. (Illustration 7-L) shows some leading pointers.

SECRET: You can get accurate angles on the lead by cutting one side at a time.

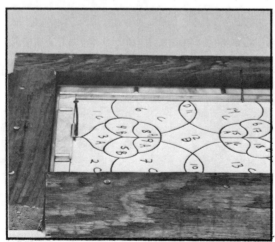
7-J Using nails to hold the work in place.

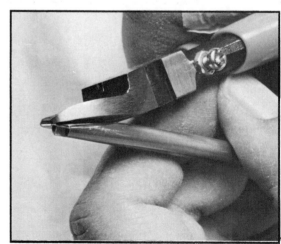
7-K Cutting one channel at a time for sharp points.

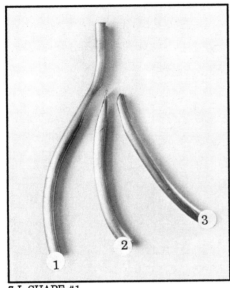 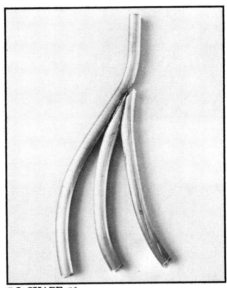

7-L SHAPE #1   7-L SHAPE #1

The main objective of these illustrations is to show the importance of cutting the lead at an angle to follow the contours of the pattern. This insures a clean, well fitting joint to solder.

Three lead pieces meet to form a point.

PIECE 1 is continuous as it passes the point, and is trimmed flat on the inside channel.

PIECE 2 is trimmed into a VERY sharp point on both sides of the channel.

PIECE 3 is trimmed at two angles on one side to meet both the previous pieces.

This shape is an exercise in deciding which piece of lead should be continuous. Choose the lines which are designed to be most flowing.

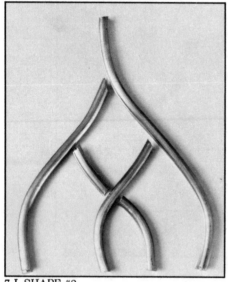

7-L SHAPE #2

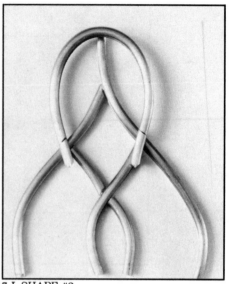

7-L SHAPE #2

The next step is to place the lead on top of the previous lead to determine the angle to cut.

(See Illustration 7-M).
This shape contains a round jewel. When leading ovals or circles, lead them with ONE continuous piece of lead.

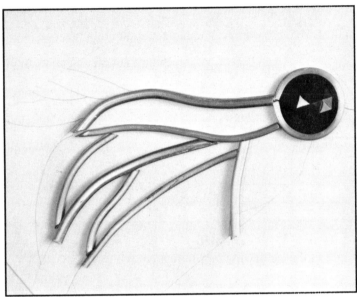

7-M SHAPE #3

The other pieces of lead (See Illustration 7-M) shows the effects of using different **widths** of lead within the *same* pattern.

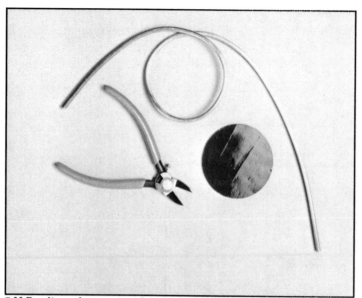

7-N Bending a larger piece for a smooth line.

SECRET: The round lead will be smoother if you gently bend a larger piece first, then cut to fit. See illustration 7-N.

LESSON EIGHT: CUTTING GLASS FOR COPPER FOIL

The internal design is going to be COPPER FOILED. Take out your foil and look at it. You will notice that when the paper backing is peeled off, the copper is sticky underneath. This foil tape will be wrapped around the edges of the glass and pressed down to give the glass a "metal edge". We'll go into the actual foiling of the glass later, but this explains why we are going to use the foiling shears to cut the pattern. The foiling shears have two blades that cut down over a middle blade. This middle blade allows a thin piece of paper to be removed from between the pieces, thus allowing room for the copper foil. (Lead pattern shears work in the same way, leaving a wider space for lead).

You should be working now with the copy of the pattern you are building on. (This is your WORKING PATTERN) The straight edges of the outside pieces will have to lay in the channel of the border lead. If you did *everything* *perfectly*, and if I drew the black line *perfectly*, then you should be able to cut along the inside of the black line (of the border) and the glass will fit *perfectly* into the channel! Fat chance, huh? The bad news (and the good news) is that "perfect" doesn't apply to stained glass...or any other art form that I know of. In this case there are too many variables--for example, how far you stretched the lead affects the width of the core. In this case the easiest thing to do is measure from the inside of the lead channels and adjust the WORKING PATTERN (See Illustration 8-A).

The measure should be accurate **but not tight.** Remember that a peg the same size as a hole won't slide in! Cut the pattern out around the outside square, to the size you have determined is accurate.

If you purchased any streaky or opal glass, mark the direction you want the streaks to run on the WORKING PATTERN. (See Illustration 8-B).

Now use your pattern shears to cut out the rest of the pattern. You will find that the shears cut best with short cuts, opening and closing them often. Try to cut the longest lines

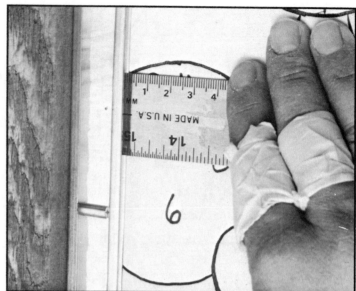

8-A Measure the panel from the inside of the lead and adjust the Working Pattern. Note the use of metric for accuracy.

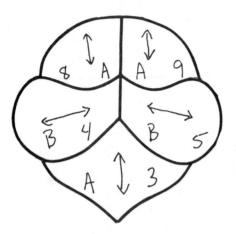

8-B Numbers, Colors and Streak direction are marked.

continuously, without turning until necessary. Sharp turns are hard to make without tearing the paper; to change directions you will need to remove the shears and re-insert them in the new direction. Keep the middle of the line in the middle of the shears so that you are removing the line.

SECRET: To keep the spray from scattering the small pieces, take a piece of excess paper and spray it with adhesive. Allow the adhesive to dry until tacky and place the pattern pieces upside-down on the adhesive.

You are going to place the pattern pieces on the appropriate glass for cutting. You don't want the pieces slipping around, so spray the backs with spray adhesive.

Spray the pattern. Wait again for the glue to get tacky, remove the pattern pieces, and place on the glass. You may remember from Lesson 6 that glass should be cut on the smooth side. Position the pattern pieces so that they can be cut apart easily, and so that the hardest cuts can be made first (See Illustration 8-C).

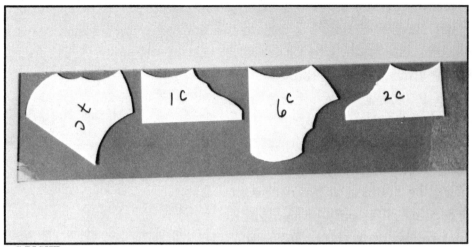

8-C RIGHT.

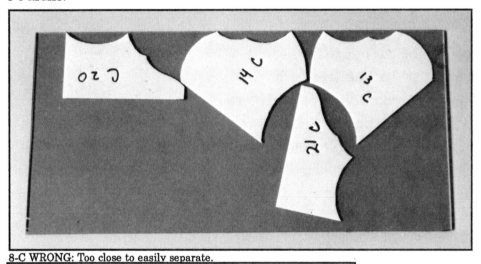

8-C WRONG: Too close to easily separate.

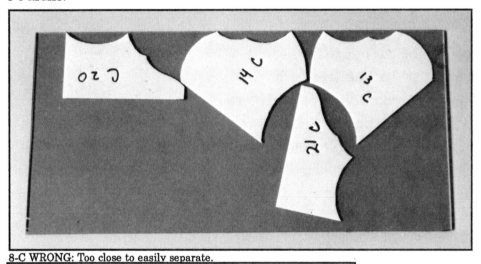

8-D With a few easy curves, the glass separates on necessary scores.

When you are comfortable with cutting strategy you can pick up some of the primary and secondary scores while separating the glass (See Illustration 8-D).

When you are working on actual fitted pieces, accuracy is **very** important. If you are still having trouble scoring on the line, and you haven't solved this with watching the line (as in LESSON 2) then try this:

Extend your thumb until it touches, but DOES NOT PUSH ON the cutting hand (See Illustration 8-E).

Your stabilizing hand can slide and rotate to maintain contact. Practice this and you will be amazed at how accurate you will become. The only precaution to take is not to lean into the stabilizing hand or push with it...you still have to keep the cutter vertical.

The glass can be cut out with the pattern on it; or you can trace around the pattern and remove the paper before cutting. I prefer cutting on an ink line so I won't get the cutter tangled up with the paper. Many professionals do leave the pattern on the glass, so the choice is yours.

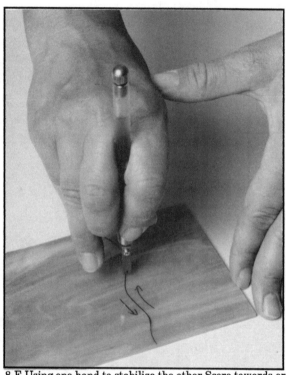

8-E Using one hand to stabilize the other. Score towards or away from yourself, but never score the same line twice!

SECRET: Your hand will be steadier if it has a stabilizing point. Place your other hand, fingertips down, on the surface beside your cutting hand.

SECRET: For pieces that cannot be gripped easily, remove the pattern piece, mark the point you want to grind to and then grind.

Go ahead and cut out the glass. Refer to Lesson 4 if you need coaching. You may have elected to get a grinder, and you will find it useful in the "fine tuning" of the pieces. "To cut or to grind?" is a question that is best approached by cutting WHENEVER POSSIBLE. If there is enough glass to grip with pliers, go ahead and score (if necessary) and break off.

The water from the grinder will make the pattern slip around, and damage it. Make it a rule to ALWAYS mark the line you want to grind to...you only *think* you'll remember where to stop! You can also use the grinder to gently buff the edges of all the pieces. This is a good idea, as it gives the foil a nice, flush edge to stick to.

CAUTION: Antique glass can be chipped by the grinding wheel, especially if the wheel is new! Grind Antique slowly, pushing gently. Clean the water off this glass immediately, as the glass dust can scratch it.

If you do not have a grinder available,

> *SECRET:* The grinding and buffing of glass is one of the most vulnerable of steps for your fingers. Use masking tape on your fore fingers and thumbs to avoid cutting them as you push on the sharp edges.

don't despair! Your local Stained Glass Studio will probably rent you time on theirs. While working at home, remember that Stained Glass was being created long before grinders were invented. Your grozing pliers are a great tool for biting off tiny pieces of glass; the inside, ribbed edge can be scraped down the edge to knock off sharp edges.

Sickle stones are an inexpensive tool that can be used to buff the edges and sand off small bumps. While I do recommend getting your own grinder, you will do well to master the grozers.

When the pieces are all cut, clean them well and lay them out on their corresponding pattern piece. With a symmetrical pattern such as this, it helps to know for sure *which* piece belongs *where* and *which side is "up"*! This will

> *SECRET:* To keep your pieces straight, mark each one with a water-proof marker (like a Sharpie or wax pen) as soon as you remove the pattern.

save you the time of playing *puzzle* with the pieces. The ink is removed easily with steel wool.

Remember the part about "perfect" not applying to Stained Glass? This is bound to be clear right about now! This is the time, however, to be a *perfectionist* about imperfection. Some of your pieces probably don't fit quite right, and may need to be altered to fit. Look at the symmetry of the pieces and check for curves that look more like snakes. Even if the pieces fit each other well, some amount of "growth" will usually occur. This is another

---

SECRET: While it is important that all pieces fit well, it is more important that the design stay constant. This means determining not only which pieces don't fit, but how to change them so they are still the right shape.

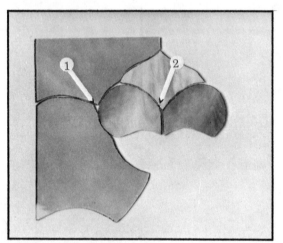

8-F The problem pieces: 1. Point is rounded. 2. Left curve starts further up than the right pieces curve.

example of "multiplied error". A 1/32" error on a curved piece can cause other

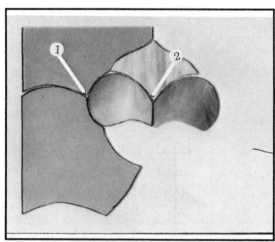

pieces to be out 1/16 of an inch. In illustration 8-F I have demonstrated the best solution to a typical problem. I hope you can see the significance of this

8-F Getting Picky pays off for the design. 1. Re-cut piece for a better point. 2. Grind curve to start lower

step in the process of building a window. While every part of the process is important, and must be attended to with care, a well cut and fitted window is a big step towards being professional quality.

8-F The original pattern.

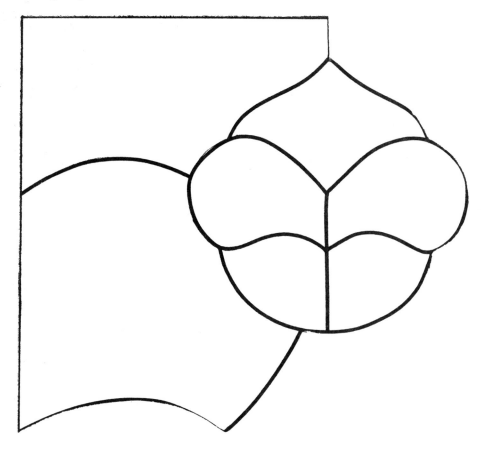

LESSON NINE:
COPPER FOILING

When all the pieces are laid out, and you are satisfied with the fit, the next step is copper foiling. BE SURE THE GLASS IS CLEAN. Foil won't stick to glass that has grinding dust, dirt, or even skin oil on it. It's a very good idea to not use hand lotion before cutting and foiling!

Peel back no more than an inch of the foil backing. Keep the foil sticky side up, foil side down, against your fore finger (See Illustration 9-A).

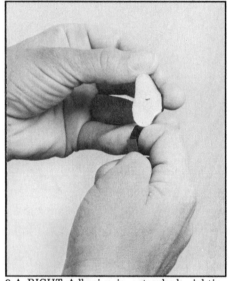

9-A RIGHT Adhesive is untouched; sighting down glass.

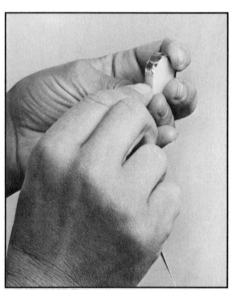

9-B WRONG Foil is between you and glass.

Sight down the glass, so that you can see the foil on both sides. Begin laying

SECRET: This will mean keeping the hand with the foil stationary, and rotating the glass. If you start moving the foil you will soon find that it comes between you and the glass.

the foil on the edge, about a half inch from a corner. Keep the glass centered on the foil by sighting down it all the way.

Remember the SECRET about not cutting anything you can't see? The same rule goes for foiling! (See Illustration 9-B).

Push firmly against the foil, so that it attaches to the edge with no gaps. Push down the foil as you complete each side of the glass. This is called "crimping" the foil.

> **SECRET:** Be sure that corners over lap the same way as "hospital corners" on sheets (one side is pushed down and the other side folds down over the top of the first side) do. See illustration 9-C. This will keep the adhesive side from turning up.

The solder will not stick to the adhesive!

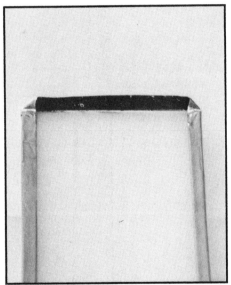

9-C RIGHT corners fold down, (Adhesive is black on this foil).

9-C WRONG adhesive is up.

> **SECRET:** If you have a deep inside curve, or mouse-hole, foil that first. Start at the deepest point of the curve, and push down the edges of the foil every quarter of an inch. The slack in the foil will help keep it from splitting, as it can fold over the top of itself instead. See illustration 9-D.

When you get back to the point where you started, overlap the foil about a half an inch.

Use the handle of the X-acto knife to smooth the foil on the edge of the glass and on both sides (See Illustration 9-E). This "burnishing" takes a little pressure; if you lay the glass down for this step be sure there are no glass chips under it. It only takes one small chip to break your hard earned glass! If you don't lay the glass down, support it well with your other hand at the point of burnishing.

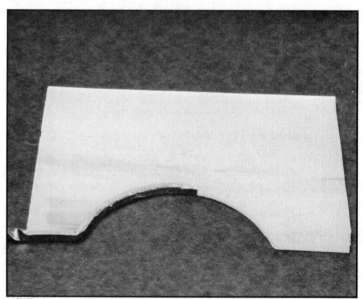

9-D Foiling inside curves from the center, crimping often.

It is possible, even probable, that some of your nice rounded curves have been squared off by the foil. Some of the straight lines may have been angled by uncentered foil (See Illustration 9-F and 9-G). Use the X-acto knife to correct the foil line. This flower petal is nicely rounded until it's foiled.

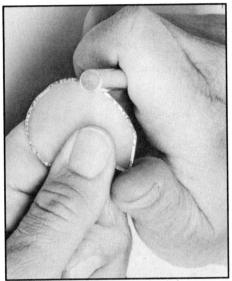

9-E Burnishing (smoothing) the foil.

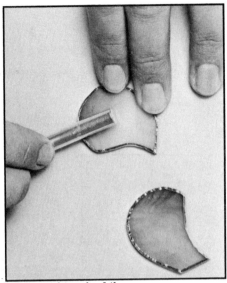

9-E Burnishing the foil

The foil line is the line that will show on the finished piece! Learning to trim foil will give your finished pieces smooth, clean lines. At times you may need to trim foil to camouflage small errors in cutting...don't tell anyone I told you to do it though!

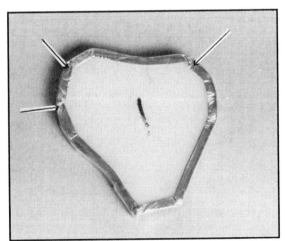

9-F Flower petal, foiled.

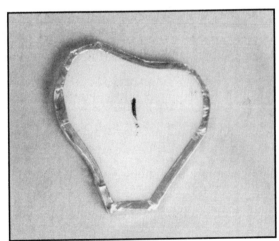

9-F Flower petal, trimmed.

A straight line has been "angled" by the foil.

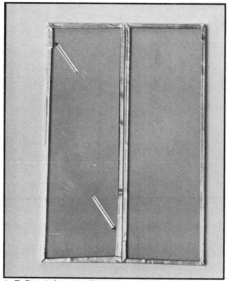

9-G Straight cut, Foiled

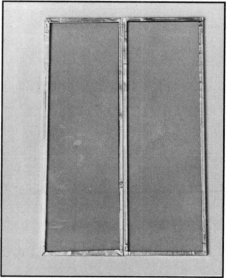

9-G Straight cut, Trimmed.

When all the pieces are foiled, place them in the lead border. Lead the top border piece in, and finish with zinc. You will notice that the top of the foiled pieces must be accurately lined up with the pattern or the border and zinc won't fit. Put nails across the top of the zinc to hold firmly in place.

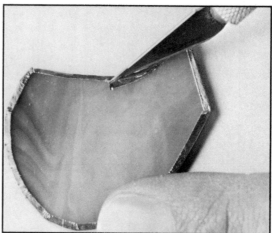

9-H You will often have to trim the overlapped foil.

LESSON TEN: SOLDERING

Are you still wearing your glasses? Remember to keep the solder and lead away from your face, and finish your lunch before you begin this process! Now open a window or door and turn on a fan if you have one. this is what is meant by that old fashioned term "well ventilated".

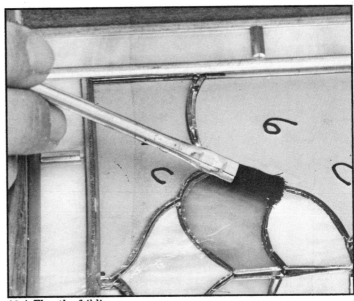

10-A Flux the foil lines.

IMPORTANT: Don't start the soldering process unless you have time to finish it. Solder doesn't like to stick to dirty flux or oxidized solder! If you must put off soldering for any length of time, cover your panel with plastic wrap.

Place a wet sponge in your soldering stand or metal ice tray. If your soldering iron came with two tips, use the larger one. Check to see if the screws holding the tip are secure. Plug in the soldering iron and put it in the stand or lay it in the tray so that it does not touch the sponge and is propped on the small stand it came with. The iron gets very hot, so place it where your hands and arms won't accidentally touch it.

Put on your rubber gloves. Use the flux brush to flux all the foil lines with liquid flux. This is not a delicate process, you just want good coverage of the foil without getting a lot of flux on the glass (some flux will, of course, be on the glass). Liquid flux tends to spatter if you use too much, or if it's too wet.

You can wait just long enough for it to dry if the spattering bothers you. This spattering is dangerous if you've forgotten your glasses!

10-A Flux the lead joints.

Flux the lead, only at the joints, with paste flux. This includes the points where the foil meets the lead. Use the paste flux on the zinc, where the lead meets it. The zinc is harder to solder, and the paste flux helps to get a good bond (See Illustration 10-A).

Take a piece of scrap lead and lay it down on the work surface. Flux a section of the lead. Now touch the lead with the tip of your iron. *OOPS!!* If your iron was heating the whole time you were fluxing, it should have melted the lead. (See Illustration 10-B).

This is a good demonstration on scrap, but lets not do it on your window. Put the tip of the iron on the wet sponge and turn it over a few times until the sizzling starts to slow down. Now repeat your test on the scrap lead. If it didn't melt immediately, then you are ready for part two of what I call the

SECRET: Your soldering iron is ready for soldering lead when it passes the first part of the test by not melting the lead, and then melting the solder immediately afterward.

"Lead Test". Unroll a 6" section of solder and dip the end in the flux. Holding it over the work surface, touch the fluxed end with the iron.

If the solder did not melt easily, wait about 30 seconds and try it again.

72

You may want to invest in a rheostat (for temperature control) at a later date, but many professionals have not found it necessary. Why is this? Because the better you get at soldering, the faster you will get, the faster you solder, the faster the heat is dispersed from the iron. You will find that by working quickly, the iron has trouble staying *hot* enough for you.

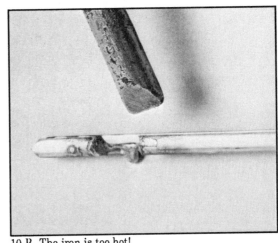
10-B The iron is too hot!

Hold the roll of solder in one hand and the soldering iron in the other (your preferred hand). How should you hold the soldering iron? There's only one hard and fast rule: ***hold it by the handle.*** Other than that, whatever is comfortable for you is fine. The unrolled end of the solder will be between the iron and the lead or foil, or zinc. Lets start with the zinc. Do not be concerned with the iron being too hot for zinc (See Illustration 10-C).

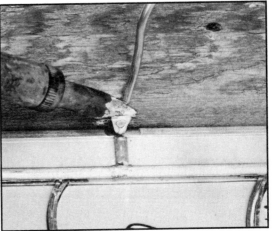
10-C Do not Drip the solder

If the tip is clean, then a hot iron is best. The tip of your iron may start to get a black "crud" on it after awhile. Just dip the hot tip into the paste flux and wipe immediately on the wet sponge. Try this a couple of times, and if the tip is still cruddy, use a wire brush on the fluxed, hot tip. If your iron was pre-tinned, don't file the tip or you'll ruin the tin coating. When the tip is clean, dip it in the paste flux and apply a little solder to both sides.

SECRET: Solder attaches to solder easier than to anything else.

Now, if your iron is hot and clean, melt the solder on the zinc only. Joining

10-D Tinning the zinc.

the lead to the zinc is easy once the zinc has a good adherence of solder on it (this is called "tinning" the zinc). Tinning should be used any time you are attaching metals that require different levels of heat. ie. Zinc must be soldered with a hot iron, and lead needs a cooler iron. Don't be afraid to touch the zinc with your iron; you will need to get the zinc pretty hot to have a good bond. If the solder cools to a very dull finish, the zinc was probably too cool. Flux it and re-melt. The solder on the zinc should have squared edges and be slightly wider than the lead (See Illustration 10-D). Repeat at every place the lead meets the zinc.

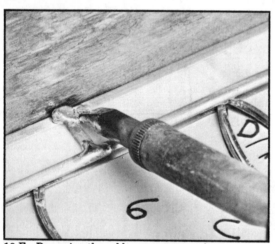

10-E. Removing the solder at a cross angle.

Now let's solder the lead. Begin with a "lead test" (always). The object of this soldering is to get an even, symmetrical solder joint. This is easiest to achieve by making small circles with the iron tip (wedge flat) at the center of each joint.

Use the solder sparingly, it's easier to add it than to remove it! What if you have too much solder on the joint?

SECRET: Use a cool iron and drag it across the joint at a cross angle. Some of the solder will follow the iron onto the glass; since you left the joint at a cross angle, you should not disturb the symmetry. See illustration 10-E.

It's all right if some of the solder remains on the glass (not attached to the lead). When it cools you can remove it with the X-acto knife. It's important to move the iron quickly during this; the glass will fracture under too much heat!!! If you still need to remove solder after about three quick tries, go on to another joint and come back after the joint cools.

Quickly pick the iron straight up and wipe on the wet sponge.

SECRET: Keep moving from joint to joint; if you pause too long the iron will heat up and your lead may do a disappearing act!

There are products such as a solder syringe and solder wicks that help in removing excess solder. If excess solder is a problem for you, ask your supplier if they carry these tools and for a demonstration.

10-F Melted lead.

10-F Beaded bridge.

10-F Smoothed once.

10-F Smoothed and blended.

Suppose you *do* melt a lead joint. It's not practical to take the window apart to replace the damaged section. Allow these beads to cool. Come back to the beads with a slightly warmer iron and solder over the top of them.

> **SECRET:** Cool your iron until it will barely melt the solder. Melt small beads of solder to form a bridge over the melted area.

Allow the area to cool for about 30 seconds and solder once more. If you never allowed the iron to get very hot, this last application of solder should flow at a level with the lead and blend at the edges (See Illustration 10-F).

The soldering iron will need to be a little hotter for the copper foil. The solder should melt smoothly without your feeling that you are pushing the solder onto the foil. If you are having to push on the solder, or the solder is rippling instead of flowing, stop and let your iron heat up. As with lead and zinc, the flat wedge of the iron should touch the foil. Many beginners try to "paint" the solder on with short strokes. Put the flat side of the iron's tip in the foil line, and feed the solder into the tip as you quickly follow the foil lines. Your result should be a gently rounded "bead" of solder (See Illustration 10-G).

If the seam of the foil shows, or the solder appears flat, you should move a little slower and use more solder. If the solder appears to flow out onto the glass or is too thick at the joints, you have used too much solder (See Illustration 10-H).

To remove some of the solder, you can re-heat the problem area and move some to the solder onto the un-soldered lines. If there are no adjoining foil lines to bring it onto, then heat the line (a little at a time)

> **SECRET:** As much as possible, fix the "blobs" and other problems before you move on to the next line. The solder will flow better (and leave less ridges) if it has not cooled too long before you touch it up.

and bring the solder off onto the glass. Lift the iron straight up and wipe on the wet sponge. Just as with the lead, this has to be done quickly or you can

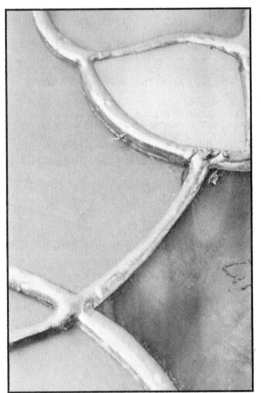
10-G Ripples mean the iron is too cool.

heat fracture the glass.

Beginners often want to solder the whole panel, and then go back and touch-up. They then find themselves touching up the touch-ups...it's no fun!

10-H Too much solder.

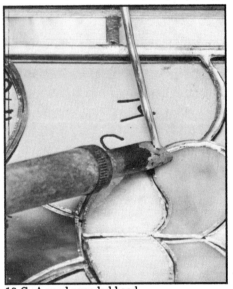
10-G A good rounded bead.

Double check to see if you missed any lines or joints. The solder should connect the lead joints with the foil lines. If you're complete with this side, remove one of the side pieces of wood. Review lesson #1 on glass safety for directions on handling the glass. Slide the panel out until half of it is over the edge of the plywood. While still supporting both edges, let the end slide down until you are holding the panel vertically (one hand under the panel, one hand on top). Spin the panel around (and sneak a peek!) and lay it back down with the other side up. Lesson #1 covers how to lay down a piece of glass.

To solder this side, repeat the steps in soldering the first side. The only real difference will be that you need to use a slightly cooler iron on the foil, or the solder will boil and leave air bubbles. Fix these by placing a cooler iron on the bubble and lifting the iron straight up. REMINDER: Don't work too long in one spot, because the glass can't take it! If your iron is too hot the solder might *melt through* to the other side. (See Illustration 10-I). Cool off your iron and re-solder these areas. You should check the first side for melt through and smooth these out (remove the extra solder if necessary).

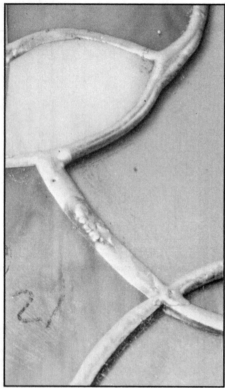

10-I Solder has melted through to other side.

LESSON ELEVEN: CLEANING THE PANEL

When both sides of the panel are soldered, and you are sure you haven't missed any joints or foil lines, you are ready for cleaning. This may sound simple, but many fine windows have been broken during this process. Take your time, be thorough and gentle, and you will do justice to all your hard work.

There must be a hundred ways to clean Stained Glass; I've heard of everything from saw dust to jacuzzi's being used! (Although I definitely wouldn't recommend the latter). I'm going to share the methods I've found to be tried and true and the least amount of hassle.

SECRET: If you have Craquel glass in your panel, cover these pieces first with clear contact paper.

If you don't, the texture will get dirty and it's almost impossible to clean; it looks like dirt under your finger nails!! Trim the contact paper to the shape of the glass so the lead/solder line will get cleaned. Remove the paper as the last step before hanging.

First, lets clean the flux off the foiled section. Wear the rubber gloves! Be sure again, that the panel is laying on a clean surface. Sprinkle plaster of Paris over the surface to be cleaned. Using the natural bristle brush, scrub the entire surface with gentle and firm strokes (See Illustration 11-A). When the plaster starts to look dirty, brush off the plaster and re-apply. This time, follow the solder lines and scrub back and forth along them until you see the glass and solder shine. Brush off the plaster into the trash.

Turn the panel over (see lesson 1 for directions) and repeat the process. Be sure the panel is completely clean and all the plaster is off. A vacuum cleaner hose with a dusting attachment works well too. Why all the fuss with the dust? The next step involves patina, which is wet...guess what happens to plaster when it gets wet?!!

KEEP YOUR GLOVES ON...this part is really hard on skin. Patina is used to darken the solder lines, so that they resemble lead or copper. Use a sponge (barely damp) to apply patina to the soldered foil lines. Some glass will

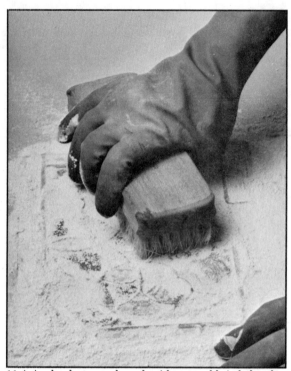

11-A Apply plaster and scrub with natural bristle brush.

become "stained" by patina, so don't just pour it on. You need to watch the solder lines as they darken. Wait until the lines turn just slightly darker than you want them, and wipe the patina off with a paper towel. Wipe until the panel is completely dry. Turn the panel over and patina the other side. Wipe dry. Now clean both sides with plaster of Paris, as you did with the flux cleaning.

Lead came that is part of a window should always be puttied. The putty fills the gap between the glass and the sides of the channel. This not only weather-proofs the panel, it also strengthens it a lot. The exception to this rule is when the lead is used as an outside edge to sun catchers and small windows. Commercially made windows may have been sent out to be "plated" to look shiny. These windows are also not puttied.

Take the (DAP 33) glass putty and add turpentine a drop at a time until it has the consistency of thick tooth-paste. Use the putty knife to mix the DAP 33. I should mention that I'm using the brand name (DAP 33) because it's the only putty I've encountered. If your supplier has a different brand, use that. Using the putty knife, place globs of putty on the lead border (See Illustration 11-B).

This will mean angling the brush into the lead lines (See Illustration 11-B).

When all the lead has been puttied on both sides, lean down and check for dark spots where the putty should be. These are the spots you missed! Remove the excess putty from the glass surface with the nail brush.

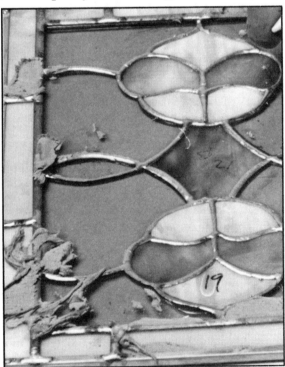
11-B Put putty on each of the leaded areas.

Sprinkle plaster of Paris on the leaded areas and scrub to remove the excess putty.
Keep the scrub brush flush with the glass so you aren't cleaning the putty under the lead! The lead will darken from the oils in the brush and putty, giving it a natural patina. As the window ages, the lead will darken even more.

SECRET: The natural bristle brush will not scratch and polish the lead like plastic bristles will.

When the leaded area looks clean, brush off the plaster into the trash. Stand the window up on edge and look for areas you may have missed. For sharp corners and lead lines, run a lead pencil (hold it vertical!) along the lead lines removing the stubborn putty spots.

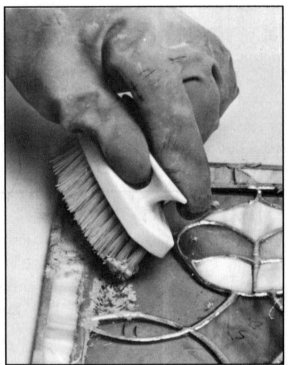

11-B Put putty on each of the leaded areas. Use the nail brush to force the putty under the edges of the lead.

> **SECRET:** The lead and solder are naturally oily. Using regular glass cleaner usually leads to oily streaks on the glass. The dry cleaning method is your best bet.

A dry cloth is the best bet for small touch ups.

Hold up your window and enjoy the beauty that only light can give glass!
CONGRATULATIONS ON FINISHING!

LESSON TWELVE:
SECRET METHODS FOR CUTTING PATTERNS

SECRET SECRET SECRET SECRET SECRET

That should about cover the whole chapter. The pattern method we covered with the first window is the traditional and most widely used method for cutting stained glass pattern shapes. The advantages are evident: 1) The pieces can be laid out on glass to use the glass efficiently 2) Since each pattern piece is cut apart from another, the fit should be good 3) Time is used well, as all the cutting is done at once.

There are other methods used by many professionals that can benefit you greatly, as they have advantages of their own!

TRANSPARENCY METHOD

A light-box is very useful for this method, but if you don't have one yet we can work around it. Your supplier can get you one with a grid top or you can make your own. Instructions for building a simple light box are at the end of this lesson.

Use PATTERN 2 for this method. Choose quality glass; there aren't many pieces to this window, but the cuts are challenging. Ask your supplier for advice on glass that is not *dense or brittle*. You will notice that this pattern does not have a straight outer edge. This will give us the opportunity to cover the building of odd shaped windows as well as the Transparency Method.

Start with a clean work surface, and cover it with white paper as you did in the first panel, and tape the paper down. Tape a copy of PATTERN 2 securely to the work surface. If you are using the board as a cutting area, mount the pattern to one side to leave room for cutting (See Illustration 12-A).

Start at the bottom of the window. If the glass you chose for piece is able to be seen through, lay it on top of the pattern and trace the shape with the fine tip marker (See Illustration 12-B).

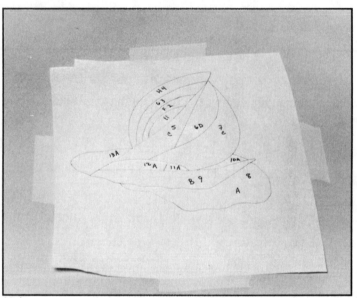

12-A

Cut the piece, smooth or grind, and foil it. **IMPORTANT;** Begin foiling all pieces on an edge that will be touching another piece of glass. If the foil overlaps on an outside edge, it may come off while soldering! Lay the next piece of glass for piece on top of the first piece. The glass will lay at an angle, so put a piece of scrap glass under the top of it and trace the shape. This second shape will have one side drawn to conform to the first glass! (See Illustration 12-C).

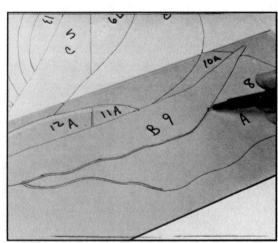

12-B Tracing through the glass.

SECRET SECRET SECRET

What if you can't see through the glass?   You have three choices.

CHOICE 1: Lay apiece of clear glass over the pattern and trace as described in the previous paragraph. To get an accurate tracing, you need to stand above the glass and look directly down at the pattern. Put the clear glass on a light box, or hold it up to a bright light, and trace the shape to the stained glass. At first this may sound tedious, but in time you will find that it can be faster than cutting with pattern shears and fitting the pieces later. The pieces have a

better chance of fitting well if they are drawn to fit each other (See Illustration 12-D).

Let me interrupt this lesson for a moment. This method is **NOT** a way of justifying being sloppy. The pieces should still look like the pattern and fit to each other well! What the Transparency Method *does* offer is the chance to compensate for the natural "growth" that happens when fitting glass.

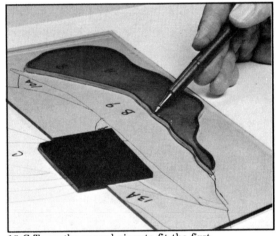

12-C Trace the second piece to fit the first.

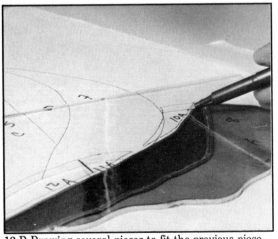

12-D Drawing several pieces to fit the previous piece.

CHOICE 2: Slide a piece of paper under the first piece of glass and trace the pattern piece. One side of the traced pattern will be traced along the edge of the first piece of glass. Cut this pattern out on the inside of your black line (the pattern will have no black line on it) (See Illustration 12-E). Spray this pattern piece with spray adhesive, and put it on the stained glass. Cut the piece as we did in Lesson 8.

CHOICE 3: Listen-up! This choice will save you loads of time if you have pieces of the same glass that fit together. It applies to both opaque and transparent glass. Take for example, your average flower.

The petals have gentle curves for sides that can easily be cut apart from each other. You can trace them, several at a time, onto the glass and cut them apart from each other. If you need to, you can use carbon paper to transfer the tracing to the glass. There are yellow wax pens available from your supplier if you are working with dark glass. Once the edges are smoothed or ground, the pieces should fit perfectly. The minor amount of "growth" that occurs can be compensated for with the next tracing. (See Illustration 12-F).

Okay, back to our sail boat: To keep the glass pieces from sliding, use lead came scraps with nails against them. When you get several pieces together, you can solder-tack. "Solder-tack" means fluxing a very small area of foil and putting just a drop of solder on it. It is important to use the minimum of flux, as you don't want it on your hands or the un-foiled glass...copper foil won't stick to flux! (See Illustration 12-G).

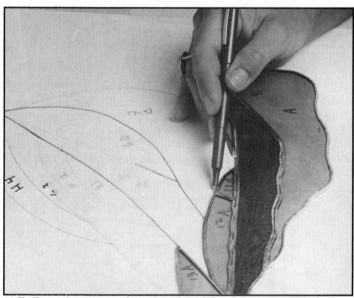

12-E Trace the pattern along the edge of the glass. Cut off black line.

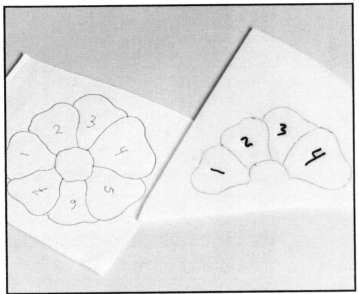

The whole window can easily be built using one of these methods. To make the project even more interesting, here's one of my favorite techniques.

12-F A flower with petals made of the same opal glass.

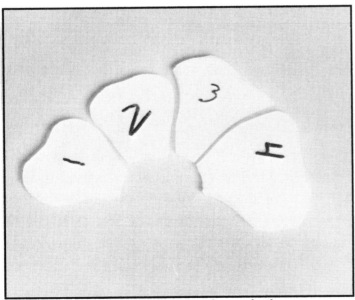

12-F Cut the pieces, a few at time, apart from each other.

I often use this method when the pieces, for the most part, are not the same color. Slip a piece of paper under the cut and foiled piece. Trace the ajoining four pieces. With regular scissors, cut the black line off the edge that borders the existing piece. Use foil shears on the rest of the lines. Spray mount the pieces to their corresponding glass and cut, smooth, fit and foil. Lay these pieces

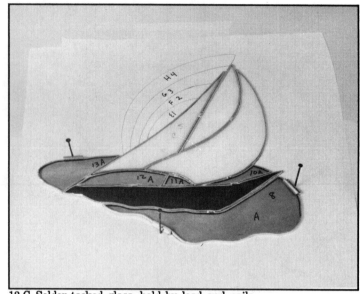

12-G Solder tacked glass, held by lead and nails.

out and solder-tack. Now slip a piece of paper under this work and trace pieces the next three or four pieces. Repeat the process.

The benefits of this method are apparent: You get the *ease* of the pattern method with the *adjustability* of the Transparency Method! The trick is to trace only a few pieces at a time. You should also be aware of tracing pieces together that share a boundary (like 8 and 9), so that they join smoothly.

This is a good time to cover cutting VERY small, long points. Keep this in mind: If the crimped foil will cover the whole glass point anyway, what is the point of cutting it? Assuming that the foil isn't too wide for the project, and that you trim off a reasonable amount of the foil as it goes to the thin point: A long point under 1/8 of an inch wide will be unnecessarily difficult to cut and is likely to heat fracture while soldering (See Illustration 12-H).

Finish cutting the panel using any of the *secret* cutting methods. Solder tack all the pieces and remove the nails and lead. If you want to trim the foil along the "mast" so that it's tapered, you can do that now. Flux and solder the panel.

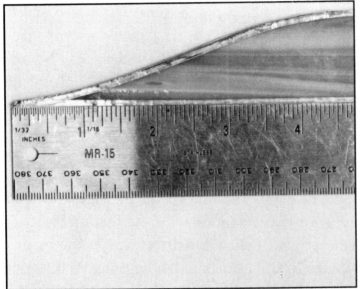

12-H This point is hard to cut, and ends up covered by foil for 3/4 in.

To finish the edges, turn the panel on it's side and use a cool iron to flow solder along the edge. You will need to do this a little at a time, giving the solder time to cool before you turn it. Be sure both sides of the foil are tinned before you start the edge. To hang the sail boat, you will need a metal ring. These can be purchased or you can make your own. Use either copper or galvanized steel wire,. By wrapping the wire around a pencil you can make hundreds of rings.

Whenever you use wire for rings or decorative work, allow about an inch of waste at the end. This will give you a much smoother line than trying to bend the end to shape. (See Illustration 12-I).

The same principle applies to shaping lead and zinc. Hold the metal from the edges and bend the middle. Trim off the ends for a graceful curve.

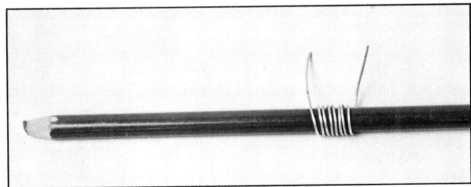

12-I Allowing a little waste will make the curve much smoother.

Cut off two of the rings and tin them. Close the ring if it is open. Hold a ring with your pliers with the closed end down and solder the closed end to the mast at the top of yellow line. The top of the ring should extend above the sail. Turn the boat over and apply the other ring in the same spot. Notice that the rings are not attached to the outer edge, where they would pull the foil away. They are located at a point where three foil lines come together, giving the rings strength. (See Illustration 12-J).

This type of panel is best cleaned with flux remover and water. If you do use the "dry cleaning" method, be careful around the foiled edges. You don't want to brush the foil off! I'm sure you wore gloves for the flux and soldering; leave them on for the flux remover too! Follow the directions on the bottle to clean before and after the patina. NOTE: Glass finishing compound is a polish available at most suppliers. It's a nice option to help maintain the color and shine of the patina.

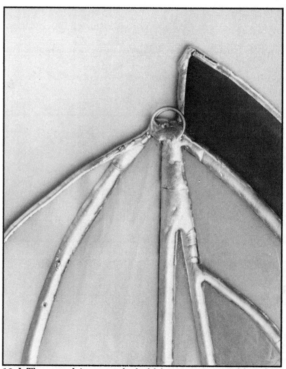

12-J The panel is securely held by two rings soldered to interior foil lines.

Hang the panel by inserting fishing line or small chain through both of the rings. Now for the last *SECRET* exercise: Raise your arm above your head, bend your elbow and give yourself a pat on the back. ***YOU DID IT!*** 90

Secret Page

(This page is not supposed to be here.
Check the Table of Contents!)

But, hey, let's have some fun with it! That's what Stained Glass is supposed to be...FUN! Now I'm going to let you in on a big *Secret*. You've only just begun! There is a lot to explore and create with in Stained Glass, and most of it is *easy* compared to what you just learned.

Etching (usually sandblasting) is a blast! And requires very little investment of time and money. Many studios have sandblasters that you can rent time on for a nominal amount. Many projects can be finished in less than a day!

Fusing. If you haven't tried fusing yet, run to the nearest phone and sign up for a workshop! The melting together of glass it really amazing and beautiful. And, like etching, the results are almost immediate. Don't believe anyone that tells you it's too technical and difficult. The glass and kiln manufactures have developed user friendly materials and equipment. You can finish a pair of fused earrings in just minutes in a "Mini Kiln"! If there is one piece of equipment that I would recommend (after a grinder, of course) it's a Mini Kiln. They are really FUN!

Stained Glass is an art form...did I say art? Did you flinch? Have you been saying "I'm just not an artist, I can't draw a straight line!" ? No problem. With the book <u>Stained Glass **Design** Secrets</u> , you can design any window even if you can't draw. And that is really adding some fun to your projects! And it is easy. Now you can say "I designed it myself." and the gift or panel will mean even more.

So, go have some fun! Create and play with your glass. Hang out in Stained Glass Studios and Galleries. Learn and evolve and most of all...never stop! Let me know how you're doing, I'd love to hear from you.

BUILDING AN EASY LIGHT BOX

You don't have to be a carpenter to build an easy light box.
You will need these materials from a large hardware/lumber store:

A WOODEN STORAGE CUBICLE. They are usually rectangular and are used to stack with other components to make wall-units. The unfinished, particle-board ones are very inexpensive.

A LIGHT SOCKET that has a base for screw-mounting, and a pull chain switch. If you can't find one with a chain, get an in-line switch.

ELECTRIC WIRE for lighting, with a good plug.

SAFETY PLATE GLASS the size of the outside dimensions of the storage cubicle. You may need to go to an auto glass store for this.

A DRILL with a variety of bits.

A SCREW DRIVER that fits the screws in the light socket.

MIRROR CLIPS You will need 6.

REFER TO THE ILLUSTRATIONS ON THE NEXT PAGE FOR EACH STEP.

Drill three 1/4 inch holes across the top half of each side of the box. These allow heat from the light to escape.

Drill a 1/4 in. hole at the bottom of one side of the wooden box. Put one end of the wire through the hole and wire the light socket according to directions. If you are not comfortable with this, go back to the hardware store and ask for help. There's no greater help than a good hardware clerk!

Mount the socket on the bottom of the box (in the middle) with the screws that it came with. This is easiest if you drill the holes first.

Wire the plug if it didn't come attached to the wire.

Lay the *safety* plate glass on top of the box and mount the mirror clips to hold it on. One option for an evenly diffused light is to paint the inside of the box and the bottom of the glass white.

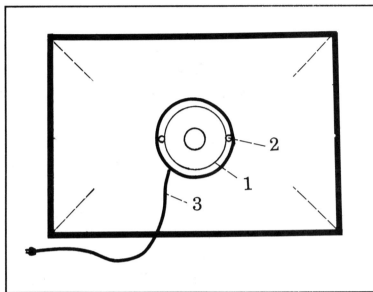

12-K Aerial view.

1. LIGHT SOCKET
2. MOUNTING SCREWS
3. ELECTRIC CORD (WITH PLUG)
4. 1/4 INCH HOLE FOR CORD
5. 1/4 INCH VENT HOLE
6. MIRROR CLIPS
7. SAFETY PLATE GLASS

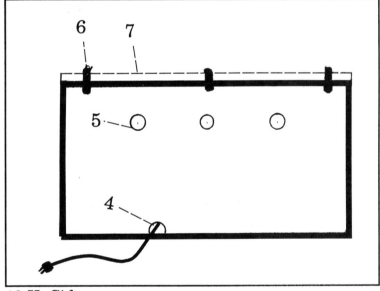

12-K Side

I sincerely hope this book has been useful for you.

No book can cover everything, and no artist has all the answers. It is my goal to give to each of you at least one SECRET that will make a positive difference in your stained glass creations. If just one of these SECRETS was a help to you, then this book is a success.

TROUBLE SHOOTING GUIDE

Problems	Possibilities
Glass won't break on score.	Score only once. Check to see if cutter is vertical to glass. See if glass cutter is damaged. Check sound of score to see if it is too light or too heavy. Be sure the score begins and ends at the edge of the glass. Check the position of your hands and pliers--they should be close to the score. Roll your hands apart for the break, don't push and pull on the glass! For difficult cuts, try warming the glass on your light box, then cut. Very warm glass cuts and breaks well.
Small pieces of glass pop out of the score.	The score was too heavy

Problems	Possibilities
Score is too light. (can't hear score).	Practice "leaning" on glass (not pushing), for good pressure. Check wrist position--is it up? Some dense glass has a silent score; especially Opals and "high color" Antiques. Try the break anyway, and ask your supplier if this glass has a silent score. Stand up to score.
Score sounded good but won't break.	Did you score on the wrong side of Flashed Antique? Did you wait more than a minute to try the break? (Score is cold). Check the position of your hands/tools and the "roll" of the snap during breaking. Check your glass cutter for chips. Try a new cutter. Did you over-score?
Score is too heavy.	Lighten up! This isn't arm wrestling. You're pressing too hard.

Glass is crushed by Grozers.	Hold Grozers with your index finger between the handles. Even the Perfect-Bite pliers will crunch the glass if you grip too hard! Are your grozers arch side up? (They should be.) Practice running the score.
Glass breaks as you score.	There may be a glass chip under the glass. Is the glass frozen? Very cold glass can shatter while scoring!. There may have been a run in the glass already. Check carefully before scoring. Too much pressure on the score, especially on Antique glass.
Cutter "drags" as you score	Remember to oil the cutter frequently. Loosen the top of your oil cutter to allow the oil to flow. You may need a new cutter. Get a good oil cutter. You may be scoring on top of the pattern piece. Try drawing around the shape and removing the paper before scoring. Is glass dirty?

Problem	Possibility
Score is off the line.	Follow the line in FRONT of the cutter. Don't watch the cutter. Steady your cutting hand with the other hand. Turn the glass, not your hand, for the best visibility of the line. Practice for short times, daily.
Thin points of glass break.	The secondary pieces are too large for the primary piece. Cut down the background glass before breaking off.
Hand (or fingers) hurt.	Masking tape fingers before cutting. Raise wrist to help prevent tight clench on glass cutter. Practice more often to build callouses.
Straight lines don't break off well.	You may have leaned into the ruler as you scored along it.
Window "grew" despite use of pattern shears.	This is normal, especially with beginners and must be adjusted for while fitting and grinding. You may want to use the transparency method.

Problems	Possibilities
Border pieces don't line up.	Concentrate on accuracy: Use "V" to mark point. Use a fine point pen and measure at three points. For perfectionists, the metric rulers are the only way to go. Begin measuring at the #1, not the end of your ruler.
Foil won't stick to glass.	Glass is dirty. If normal cleaning won't work, try denatured alcohol mixed half with water. (Get at hardware store) Foil is dirty. DON'T touch the sticky side with your fingers!
Foil comes off glass while soldering.	Foil must be started and finished at a place where it will be BETWEEN two pieces of glass, not on an outside edge.
Foil is crooked.	Don't let the foil get between you and the glass. Rotate the glass, not the foil. Trim foil with X-acto knife.

Foil tears when trimming.	Try a new blade in your X-acto, if this happens while cutting.
	Hold the knife so that the blade is at an angle, don't cut only with the point.
	Did you get thin foil? The 1 ml foil is so thin that it's hard to trim and remove. I suggested 1.5 ml because it's user-friendly! (there are sizes in between that you may want to try).
Glass pieces don't fit.	Did you get the pieces mixed up? Number them before removing pattern piece!
	Use grinder and grozers to adjust.
	If you are using the Transparency method, hold the pen out from your fingers, so you can see the line and accurately trace.
Melted solder is dull.	Iron may be too cool.
	Work moved before solder could cool.
	Use flux!
	The iron heated only the solder, not the metal underneath. The iron should touch the work!

Problems	Possibilities
Solder "peaks" and won't flow.	Flux, flux, flux!. Be sure metal is clean. Go over the area with steel wool (not soaped!). Iron may be too cool.
Iron is hot, but won't melt solder.	Iron may be dirty; dip it in paste flux and wipe it on wet sponge. Iron tip may be loose. Unplug it and tighten set screw on iron shank.
Solder is dull around hanging ring.	The ring moved before the solder could cool. The ring wasn't tinned before soldering work.
Lead melts when soldered.	Iron is too hot. Do a lead test before soldering. Repair lead with very cool iron.
Glass breaks while soldering.	Oops! You over heated the area and heat fractured the glass. Move the iron faster. Repairing windows is a lesson of it's own! See your stained glass supplier for coaching on removing the piece.

Solder line has ripples. (On foil)	Iron may be too cool. You may be "painting" the solder on in short brush strokes. Move the iron at an even, steady pace. The tip of the iron may have been used on a corner. Use the flat side of the tip.
Solder joint has ripples. (On lead or zinc)	Try bringing the iron straight up after soldering in a small circle. Be sure the flat side of the iron is touching the metal.
Glass has adhesive residue.	Let the adhesive dry on the paper before applying to glass. Clean with denatured alcohol before foiling or leading.
Putty seeps out onto glass.	This is normal for the first few days. Use a pencil to clean up the edges. Let the putty set for two days before moving off table.

Problem	Possibility
Can't find the right design to fit the window or frame, and you can't draw your own!	No problem!!! You can design even if you can't draw with "Stained Glass **Design** Secrets"!
Patina is blotchy	Clean all flux off the solder lines before patina is applied. Give the patina time to darken before cleaning off. Don't leave patina on for more than a few minutes before cleaning.

ANTIQUE GLASS	Glass made by the blowing through molten glass with a hollow tube.
BALL TIP	Type of handle for glass cutter with ball shaped end.
BACKGROUND GLASS	Glass to be removed from the primary piece.
BEAD OF SOLDER	The melted, rounded solder as it flows on to the metal.
BEADED BRIDGE	Method for repairing melted lead with cool solder.
BEVELED GLASS	Thick glass, ground and polished around the edges.
BOARDED UP	Nailing wood strips accurately around the edges of windows to define the size.
BREAK LINES	Lead or foil lines designed to allow the pattern o be cut out of glass.
BREAKING PLIERS	Tool designed to assist in breaking off stained glass at the score.
BURNISHING	Smoothing down the crimped foil.
CATHEDRAL GLASS	Glass made by machine by rolling it on tables.
CATS PAW	An opal glass with a mottled color resembling cats paws.
CELLULOSE SPONGES	"Kitchen" type sponges that get hard when dry.
CHANNEL	The opening in came that holds the glass.
CHICKEN SCORE	Scores added to reduce the size of the background glass.
CLAW-HAMMER	Tool for hammering and removing nails.
COPPER FOIL	Copper tape used to wrap around the edges of glass pieces; for the solder to bind to.
CRAFT PAPER	Inexpensive, plain white paper for patterns.
CRAQUEL	Blown glass that has a rough texture resembling alligator skin.
CRIMPING THE FOIL	Pushing the edges of the foil down to the sides of the glass.
CUTTING OIL	Oil for lubricating glass cutters wheel.
CUTTING QUALITY	The ability of a type of glass to score and break well.
CUTTING STRATEGY	Determining the sequence of scores and breaks to best assure a successful cut.
CUTTING WHEEL	The wheel of the glass cutter.
DAP GLASS PUTTY	Putty for lead came; it seals the glass to the lead.
90 DEGREE ANGLE	The exact measure of the corner of a square.
DIFFUSED LIGHT	Light that is "spread out" evenly.
ETCHED GLASS	Glass that has been sandblasted or treated with acid to remove part of the surface.
FID	A wooden tool for burnishing copper foil and opening came channels.

FIST POSITION	The hands form a fist as they hold the glass to get a good snap.
FLASHED GLASS	Antique glass with a thin veneer of color on the main color.
FLEX	Gently bending the glass to run a score.
FLUSH SIDE	The side of the lead cutters that cuts a straight line.
FLUX	Chemical used to clean lead and foil before soldering. Comes in both liquid and paste form.
FLUX BRUSH	Small stiff brush for applying flux.
FLUX REMOVER	Chemical cleaner for washing off flux.
FOILING SHEARS	Special scissors for cutting patterns. They remove strip of paper and allows for the copper foil.
FRAME	Placing boards around patterns to keep the size accurate
FULL BLOWN	Term used to describe hand made Antique glass.
GLASS CUTTER	Tool used to score glass.
GLASS FINISHING COMPOUND	Used to polish the glass and metal.
GLASS GLOBS	Rounded glass nuggets, irregularly formed.
GLASS GRINDER	Motorized grinder, used with water, for shaping and polishing edges of glass.
GLUE CHIP	Glass that has been sandblasted and coated with warm glue. The glue adheres as it cools and shrinks, causing a "Jack Frost" crystal effect.
GROWTH	The tendency for the glass pieces to end up larger than the pattern.
GROZING PLIERS	Tool used to break off scored glass and trim edges.
"H" CAME	Strips of lead or zinc made to hold two pieces of glass in the two channels of an "H".
HEAT FRACTURE	Glass breaks if it becomes too hot.
HIGH COLOR	Very brilliant, warm colors
HORSE-SHOE NAIL	A flat sided nail.
HOSPITAL CORNERS	Folding the foil down against the glass so that no adhesive is revealed. (Ask your Mom!)
INSIDE CURVE	A shape involving removing part of circles.
IRIDESCENT	Glass that has one surface with a "mother of pearl" quality to it.
JEWELS	Faceted glass pieces, either cast or cut.
JIG	A structure of "stops" designed to cut duplicate strips of glass.
KNUCKLE-ROLL	Method of achieving a good snap in breaking off scores.
L-SQUARE	Tool for measuring 90 degree angles; shaped like an L.
LEAD CAME	Lead strips with open channel to hold glass.
LEAD CUTTERS	Plier-like tool, used to cut lead came accurately.
LEAD JOINTS	The place that two pieces of lead join to be soldered.

LEAD LINES	Lead came, as it follows the cut glass pieces to hold them together.
LEAD PATTERN SHEARS	Special scissors that remove a strip of paper to allow for the lead channel.
LEAD TEST	A way to determine if the Iron is too hot for lead.
LEAD VICE	Tool used to hold the lead came while it is being stretched.
LIGHT BOX	Lit box used to see through glass.
MACHINE BLOWN	Term used to describe machine blown Antique glass.
MIRROR CLIPS	Small plastic clips to hold the safety glass on top of the light box.
MOLTEN GLASS	Glass that has been heated to a liquid state. By the way, ALL glass is really still liquid!
MOUSE-HOLE	Inside curves, removing half circles from glass.
OPAL(OPALESCENT)	Glass that cannot be seen through easily.
OPAQUE	Glass that is too dense to see through.
OUTER BAR	Came used on the outside edge of panels.
OUTSIDE CURVE	A cut involving an obtuse, rounded shape.
OXIDANTS	An element or chemical that causes oxygen to react with metal and discolor it.
SEEDY	Glass with air bubbles in it.
PATINA	Chemical used to darken solder.
PATTERN METHOD	Method of cutting stained glass using paper pieces of pattern for a guide.
PLASTER OF PARIS	Dry plaster dust used to clean panels.
PLYWOOD	Used to build stained glass panels on.
POINT	The ends of an inside score.
PRIMARY PIECE	The glass in the shape of a pattern piece.
PRIMARY SCORE	The score that follows the line of the pattern piece.
REAMY	Heavily textured glass, usually Antique, that looks like it has been stretched.
RHEOSTAT	A tool used to control the heat of soldering irons.
RONDELLES	Round glass "plates" with a spiral shape.
RULE OF MULTIPLIED ERROR	An error in measuring straight lines becomes a greater error as the line gets longer.
RUN	A fracture in the glass, hopefully on the score.
RUNNING PLIERS	Tool used to flex glass and cause a run on the score.
SAFETY GLASSES	Clear glasses worn for protection.
SCORE	A scratch in the glass, made by a glass cutter, that allows the glass to break along it.
SECONDARY SCORE	A score that is across background glass, meant to give the Primary score a path to break off in.
SHADOWING	Leaving a thin layer of glass as the last background glass to be removed from an inside curve.

SHARPIE	Type of felt tip marker that is not water soluble. Used to mark the piece numbers on glass.
SICKLE STONE	Long stone for hand-grinding the edges of glass.
SMOOTH SIDE	The side of textured glass with the least texture (the side to score on.)
SNAP	Term used to describe a good breaking of stained glass.
SOLDER	Meltable metal, usually lead and tin, used to bond lead and copper foil together.
60/40 SOLDER	Solder made up of 60% tin and 40% lead.
SOLDER SYRINGE	Tool for removing excess solder.
SOLDER TACK	Keeping the foiled pieces of glass together by soldering in very small area.
SOLDER WICK	Braided wire for removing excess solder.
SOLDERING IRON	Used to melt solder; available in variety of wattage.
SOLDERING IRON TIPS	The removable tip of the soldering iron.
SOLDERING STAND	Metal holder for soldering iron.
SQUARE ANGLE	Exactly 90 degrees.
STAINED GLASS	Glass of any color, made for decorative purposes.
STREAKY	Glass with moderate to heavy streaks of color in it.
STRESS LINES	Lines in the glass caused from the blowing process.
SUN CATCHERS	Small, unframed panels. Usually with irregular sides.
SURFACE TENSION	A smooth, unbroken surface.
TANGENTS	Secondary scores that join outside curves in as straight a line as possible.
TAPERS	Shapes that thin down to points.
THREE POINT RULE	To get an accurate measure, you must measure in at least 3 places.
TIFFANY	Referring to Louis Tiffany, a pioneer of stained glass art, especially with copper foil.
TRANSPARENCY METHOD	Method of cutting stained glass by tracing the pattern directly on to the glass.
TRANSPARENCY-PATTERN METHOD	A method of cutting stained glass using tracing paper to build the pieces against each other.
TRIM	Using an X-acto knife to get the foil to the desired shape.
TRIM WOOD	Very straight quality strips of wood.
TURPENTINE	Used in place of cutting oil for lubricating glass cutter's wheel.
"V"-MARK	A method of measuring using "V"s instead of dots.
WAX PEN	Used to mark on dark glass.
WIRE CUTTERS	A plier like tool used to cut thin metal.
WISPY	A lightly streaked glass.
WORKING PATTERN	The pattern copy that is cut up during the pattern method.

X-ACTO KNIFE   Name of a razor sharp knife useful with copper foil.

ZINC CAME   Strips of zinc with shaped channels to hold glass. Used to strengthen panels.

ABOUT THE AUTHOR

ALICIA LARSON has been a Stained Glass artist since 1975. She was co-owner of Minturn Stained Glass in Minturn, Colorado until 1978, when she opened Crystal Images Stained Glass in both Vail and Minturn, Colorado. Specializing in custom original design, her work is displayed from Australia and England to the Orient.

Director of the Stained Glass Department at Colorado Mountain College in Vail for three years, she also coordinated and taught stained glass classes for the Summer-Vail Workshops during that time.

A few of her original designs can be seen in Hidden House Publication's book "Stained Glass Vistas", where one of her windows was also awarded the back cover photograph.
Now a resident of Park City, Utah, Alicia works in her studio the "Hot Glass Gallery". Her other books include Stained Glass **Design** Secrets and Stained Glass Anatomy.

Introducing:
Crystal Images'
Stained Glass Glue™

"The *clearest* choice in stained glass glue."

Crystal Images' Stained Glass Glue was developed as the first *all purpose glue* for glass artists. Alicia Larson, author of <u>Stained Glass Secrets,</u> and <u>Stained Glass Design Secrets,</u> found she needed a very clear laminating glue for her art work. After months of testing and development, she was delighted to find a glue that not only dried **clear and strong** for laminating glass together, but also doubled as a **virtually invisible** fusing glue!

How to Use **Crystal Images' Stained Glass Glue**tm

Mosaic: Cut scrap glass into small pieces. Put clear glass over your pattern. Arrange the colors of stained glass within the lines of your pattern until you like the shapes. The glass should not fit perfectly together, but should generally follow the curves of your pattern. Glue the small pieces as directed for laminating. Allow the glue to dry **completely.** Apply grout to fill in the spaces of your mosaic stained glass art. This is a great way to use up all those small pieces of expensive glass you've been saving!

Laminating: Apply evenly over surface of glass to be glued. Press to surface of clean glass. Allow to dry. Excess may be washed off while wet. (Water resistant when dry.) Use this to glue a smooth jewel or small piece of glass that requires no lead lines. Polish those sharp edges first!

Fusing: Apply sparingly <u>near edges</u> of glass. (This will avoid "trapping" the glue when the glass slumps!) Glue smaller pieces to *clean* larger pieces. Glue will fuse clear on fully fused glass.

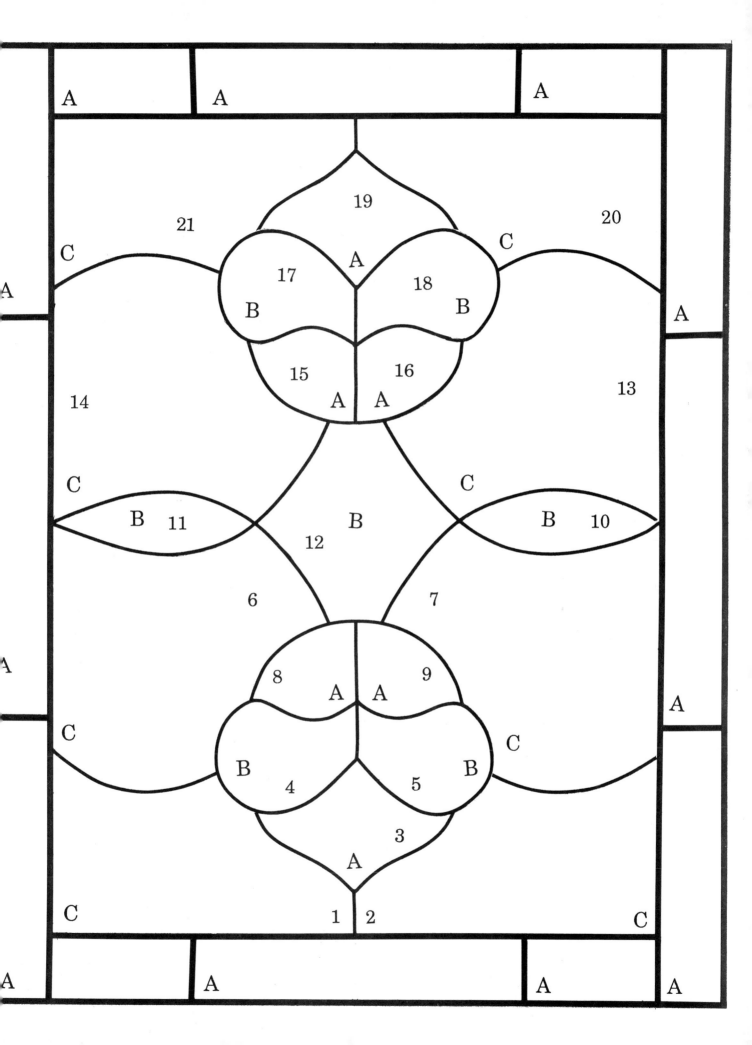

PATTERN 1:

COLORS	SIZE *
A-Light pink or irridescent white opal.	1.5 sq. ft
B-Lt. blue opal	.5 sq. ft.
C-Clear pastel green	1.5 sq. ft.

Sizes allow for some repeat cuts.

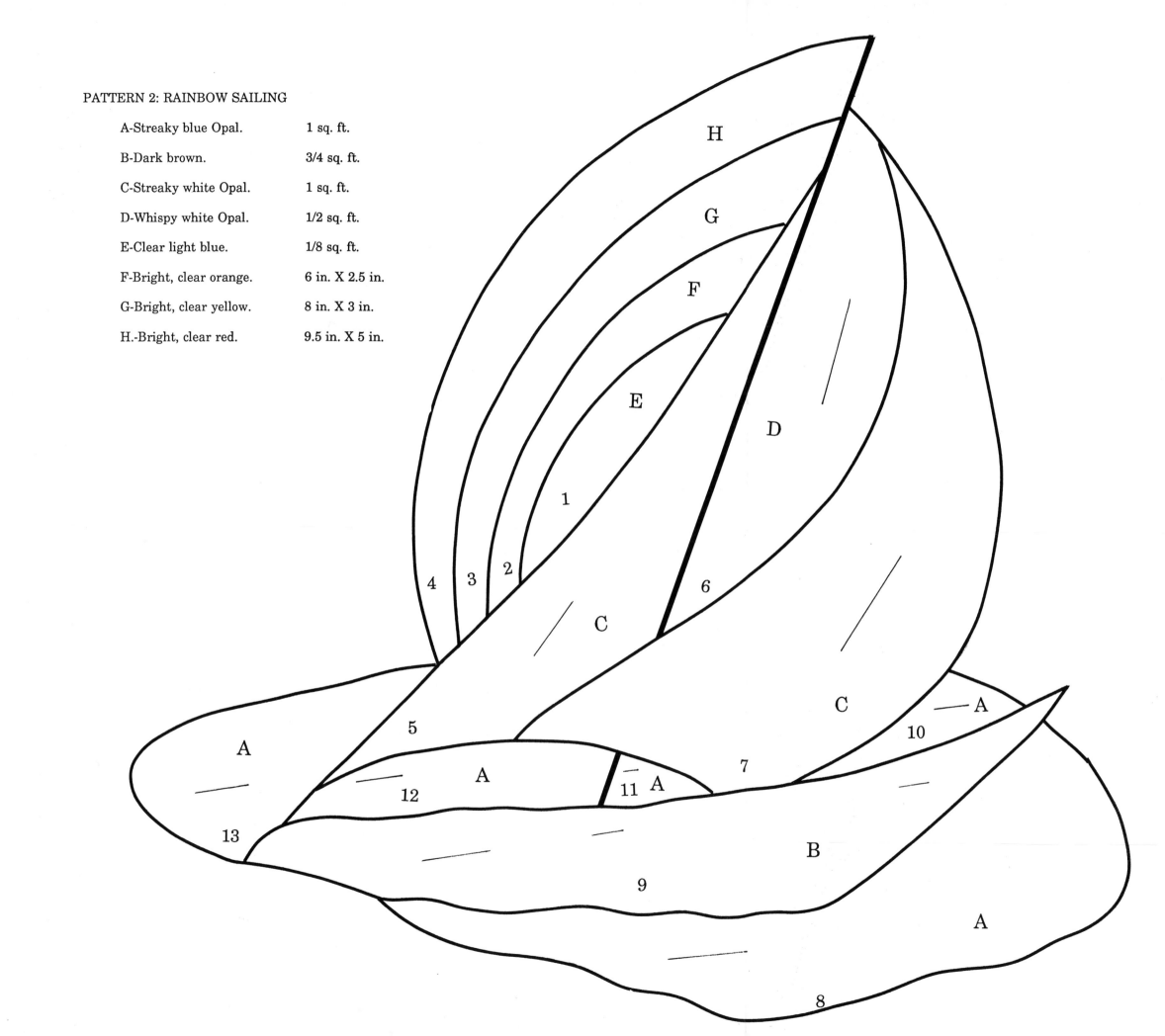

PATTERN 2: RAINBOW SAILING

A-Streaky blue Opal.	1 sq. ft.
B-Dark brown.	3/4 sq. ft.
C-Streaky white Opal.	1 sq. ft.
D-Whispy white Opal.	1/2 sq. ft.
E-Clear light blue.	1/8 sq. ft.
F-Bright, clear orange.	6 in. X 2.5 in.
G-Bright, clear yellow.	8 in. X 3 in.
H.-Bright, clear red.	9.5 in. X 5 in.

Psssssst... Wanna Hear More Secrets?!!!

Look for <u>Stained Glass Secrets, Book II</u> (the Sequel)

Coming soon to a supplier near you!